MSP®

Practice

Managing Successful Programmes Study Guide

London: TSO

List of figures

Foreword

In today's world where change seems ever-present, *Managing Successful Programmes* (MSP®) helps organizations introduce change into their businesses, allowing them to morph and thrive in uncertain times. MSP helps organizations to deal with uncertainty, to structure their strategic responses, and to introduce and integrate new ways of working into their businesses until the new way becomes business as usual. How can individuals demonstrate that they understand the concepts necessary to deliver this change? Clearly the best way is through a strong track record of delivering change in the past, but how do you get started? One approach is to gain a recognized qualification in programme management such as MSP by taking an examination.

I must confess to never having enjoyed examinations. Laying down for scrutiny your understanding of a subject is never comfortable; and when you add to that the preparation – the hours spent poring over the guide in an attempt to understand every nuance and interpretation, while all the time trying to relate that to your experience at work – it makes for a very stressful time.

With that in mind I encouraged the creation of a study guide that would help people to prepare for the MSP examinations, not simply through repetition and rehearsal of the questions they would be likely to face, but rather from an *understanding* of the types of question and the best way to go about tackling them. We can all sympathize with the candidate who opens the exam paper and wonders, 'Just what are the examiners getting at?' or simply, 'What is it they are asking?'

This publication is designed to supplement either formal training in a classroom or self-study at home by helping you to understand what the examiners are trying to convey and the best way to answer the various question types. As far as possible the authors have been asked to provide the sort of friendly advice that a 'kindly but knowledgeable relative' might give, and I hope that you will find this approach useful in preparing for your exam. Hopefully, it will help to lower your stress levels!

Finally, whichever learning route you have chosen, let me wish you all good luck in preparing for your exam(s) and in applying MSP in your future roles.

Mike Acaster
PPM portfolio manager
Cabinet Office

Acknowledgements

The commissioners and publisher are grateful to the following for their contribution to the development of this study guide.

AUTHORS

Both authors are experienced members of the MSP examination panel.

Adrian Hicks	Kalamunda Consulting Ltd
Michelle Rowland	A & J Project Management Ltd

REVIEW PANEL

We are grateful to the following people for the time and consideration they have put into reviewing drafts of this guide.

Anne Bellingan	Training consultant
David Crawford	APMG assessor and MSP examiner
Anne Gibb	Agba
Angelika Hamilton	Project management consultant/ APMG assessor
Jo Harper	APMG assessor and examiner
Geof Leigh	Goaldart Ltd

Introduction

1

1 Introduction

1.1 PURPOSE OF THIS GUIDE

This guide gives an overview of the Managing Successful Programmes (MSP) Foundation, Practitioner and Advanced Practitioner qualifications and is designed to help prepare candidates for the examinations. It reflects MSP as described in the 2011 edition of the MSP guide – *Managing Successful Programmes* (Cabinet Office, 2011).

There are study guides available for other Best Management Practice products, such as *Managing Successful Projects with PRINCE2®*. These products are complementary and cover different areas. It is important to understand that although some documents described in the various study guides have similar names, they are not exactly the same in terms of content. For example, the project business case and the programme business case, although related, have different content.

The examination regime for each of the Best Management Practice products is similar, but there are some differences and the types of question encountered may vary.

This study guide suggests ways to approach the examinations associated with the various levels of qualification, based upon the authors' experience and knowledge. It provides advice rather than instruction and is not intended as a definitive manual for tackling the examinations. While revising for the examination(s), candidates should decide for themselves what are the best methods and approaches to the various styles of question that will be encountered.

This guide contains:

- Details of the MSP examination syllabus, showing the different subject areas of MSP and learning levels which could be tested in each examination
- An outline of the format and structure of the Foundation, Practitioner and Advanced Practitioner examinations
- A description of the question types which may be included in each examination
- Samples of the types of question for the Foundation and Practitioner examinations, together with rationales for correct answers
- Hints and tips on how to address the different types of question in each examination
- Some advice on how to revise for the examinations.

This guide does not attempt to provide you with details of MSP itself, which can be found in *Managing Successful Programmes*, the official guide to MSP. That guide is essential reading for those wishing to sit the examinations and obtain any level of MSP qualification.

Other aids exist to assist in studying for the MSP examinations. Sample papers are available from the APM Group (APMG). The training provider may also supply additional materials to anyone attending a training course.

1.2 PURPOSE OF THIS CHAPTER

The purpose of this chapter is to provide an overview of MSP and its associated qualifications. It also includes information common across all the qualifications. Specific qualification-related material is included within the relevant qualification chapter later in this guide.

This chapter covers:

- **Introducing MSP** This section explains what MSP is and where it comes from.

- **MSP qualifications** This section gives an overview of each of the MSP qualifications accredited by APMG, the examining body.

- **General information** The final part of this chapter provides information that is common to several qualifications; for example, it explains how to complete the computer-marked answer booklet.

1.3 INTRODUCING MSP

MSP represents proven best practice in programme management in how to successfully deliver transformational change, drawn from the

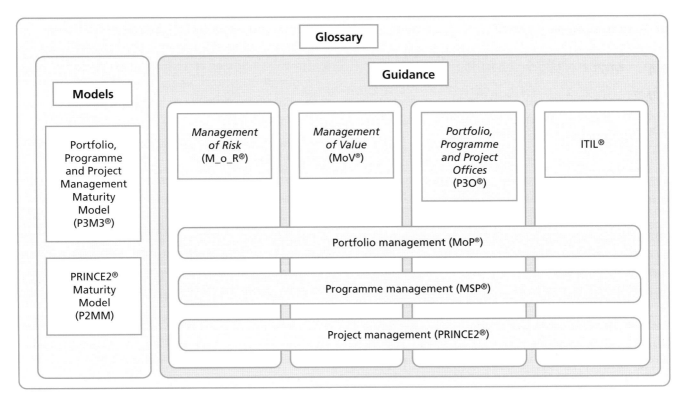

Figure 1.1 MSP's relationship with other Best Management Practice guides

experience of both public- and private-sector organizations. It is used in countries around the world, and its take-up grows daily.

MSP is part of a suite of Best Management Practice guidance, developed by the UK Cabinet Office, which is aimed at helping organizations and individuals manage their projects, programmes and services effectively. Figure 1.1 shows the structure of the set.

Where appropriate, Best Management Practice methods and guidance are endorsed by qualification schemes, and all aspects of Best Management Practice are supported by accredited training and consultancy services. Please refer to the Best Management Practice website (www.best-management-practice.co.uk) for details of other Best Management Practice publications.

1.4 MSP QUALIFICATIONS

APMG, the examination body for MSP, has offices in Australia, Benelux, China, Denmark, Germany, the United Kingdom and the United States. These offices serve the growing number of candidates across the world who want to take the MSP examinations, which are now available in English, Dutch, French and Polish.

There are three levels of MSP qualification:

- Foundation
- Practitioner
- Advanced Practitioner.

The APMG accredited qualifications at Foundation and Practitioner levels are based upon objective test examination (OTE) standards for multiple-choice papers. The Advanced Practitioner level is based upon a traditional essay style.

The Foundation level tests understanding of the principles and terminology used in MSP. The Practitioner level tests the ability of a candidate to apply and tailor MSP to address the needs and problems of a relatively uncomplicated programme scenario provided to the candidate for the first time at the time of the examination. The Advanced Practitioner level tests the ability of a candidate to adapt and apply MSP guidance in a complex programme environment.

1.5 RE-REGISTRATION QUALIFICATIONS

All MSP practitioners and/or advanced practitioners who wish to retain their registration status need to be re-registered within three to five calendar years of their original certification by re-sitting the appropriate examination.

Re-registration candidates in particular need to be aware that MSP is reviewed and revised on a periodic basis in the light of experience and changes in best practice, and examinations will be based upon the latest version of the guidance. At the time of publication of this study guide, examinations are based on the 2011 edition of *Managing Successful Programmes*.

This guide does not attempt to identify all the changes that may have occurred to MSP over time. Candidates need to ensure that their knowledge is up to date by reviewing the current MSP guide. The choice of sample questions in this study guide does, however, try to reflect any significant changes in MSP guidance.

Candidates seeking re-registration should be aware that the original three levels of qualification (known as Foundation, Intermediate and Practitioner) have been changed. Someone with the original Practitioner qualification is qualified to, and needs to apply for re-registration at, Advanced Practitioner level if they sat the old Practitioner examination. The change took place during late 2007. APMG will be able to advise candidates as to which version of the qualification they already hold, and which examination should be taken in order to re-register.

1.6 GENERAL INFORMATION

1.6.1 Conventions

Both the MSP guide and the examinations follow the use of international English. This means that words that can be spelt either with a 'z' or an 's' (for example organize/organise) are spelt with a 'z'. This guide follows a similar practice.

The MSP guide does not use capitalization for the names of documents, such as the 'risk management strategy', or the names of roles, themes and processes (with the exception of transformational flow processes); when such terms appear in normal text they are used within a context that makes it clear that a document is being referred to.

Examination questions, however, lack that context. Therefore, questions in examinations do use capitalization to assist a candidate's comprehension. This study guide generally follows the convention used in the core MSP guide, with no capitalization for MSP documents, roles, themes and processes (except transformational flow processes). However, for the sample questions and rationales, the capitalization style as applied in the examinations, rather than the MSP guide, has been adopted.

Appendix A of the MSP guide describes the typical content of various documents by providing bullet points for the information that should typically be included. In the Practitioner examination,

questions refer to each of these bullet points as 'headings' and that convention is also adopted within this study guide.

1.6.2 Answer booklet

For Foundation and Practitioner qualifications the candidate must submit their answers in the official answer booklet.

The answer booklets are read electronically and the results generated by computer. It is therefore essential that the instructions given are followed and answers indicated correctly. Failure to do so may lead to delay and, in some cases, answers being void.

All answers are given by means of the candidate filling in 'ovals' that relate to their chosen response. Figure 1.2 provides an example of a filled-in answer sheet for questions 1–4 (choosing one of five options, A–E, to respond to each question).

The only acceptable ways to complete the answer sheets are either:

- Completely filling in the oval, or
- Drawing a line through the centre of the oval, ensuring that 80–100% of the oval is filled in (see oval in Column E in Figure 1.2 for an example of this).

The oval must be filled in **in pencil, not pen**. If a pen is used, the answers may not be marked.

Any other method, including ticks or crosses, is not acceptable and may not be marked.

If a candidate wishes to change their answer during the exam, the incorrect answer should be erased completely and the correct answer indicated. If more than one answer is given by the candidate, and the question requires only one answer, the score for that question will be zero.

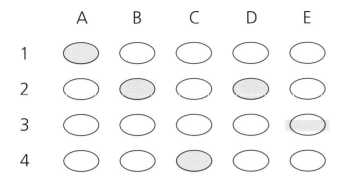

Figure 1.2 How to complete an answer sheet (example)

Hints and tips

- An easy way to fill in the ovals on your answer sheet is to draw a line around the outside of the shape first and then colour it in.
- Make sure you take a pencil and eraser into the exam with you.

The MSP syllabus 2

2   The MSP syllabus

The material in this chapter is based upon the APMG document: *MSP 2011 – Syllabus Version 2.0*. The complete syllabus is available from APMG at www.apmg-international.com

The syllabus is the document that provides detail about which topics will be examined at each examination level.

2.1   INTRODUCTION

MSP guidance explains the programme management principles, governance themes and transformational flow that should be applied to the management of programmes for transformational change in any environment.

The syllabus is based on the 2011 edition of *Managing Successful Programmes*. It addresses the requirements of assessments at all three levels of qualification, i.e. Foundation, Practitioner and Advanced Practitioner.

The syllabus provides accredited training organizations and candidates with a breakdown of all the learning level outcomes that are tested in the MSP examinations. The level at which an outcome is tested is shown by a tick in the appropriate column within the tables in the syllabus.

The syllabus describes the requirements a candidate is expected to meet in order to demonstrate that these learning outcomes have been achieved at each qualification level. As a result, it may support the development of any learning materials and should be read in conjunction with the MSP

Foundation exam candidate guidance, the MSP Practitioner exam candidate guidance and the MSP Advanced Practitioner exam candidate guidance (see 'Further information' at the end of this guide for details).

2.2   HIGH-LEVEL PERFORMANCE DEFINITION OF A SUCCESSFUL CANDIDATE

The standards expected of registered Foundation, Practitioner and Advanced Practitioner candidates are outlined below.

2.2.1   Foundation

Candidates need to show that they understand the key principles and terminology within the MSP guidance.

Specifically, successful candidates should be able to:

- Distinguish between projects and programmes
- Identify the MSP defined types of programme and their characteristics
- Explain the benefits of applying the MSP guidance to the management of a programme of transformational change
- Explain the purpose and areas of focus of the defined roles
- Explain the purpose of the seven MSP principles, the nine governance themes and the six transformational flow processes
- Explain the purpose of MSP programme information (documents).

2.2.2 Practitioner

Candidates need to exhibit the competencies required for the Foundation qualification and show that they can apply the MSP guidance in a relatively uncomplicated programme within a programme environment.

Specifically, successful candidates should be able to:

- Identify additional value as a result of managing the described change as an MSP programme
- Explain and apply each of the MSP principles, the governance themes and the transformational flow processes and their activities
- Explain the relationship between the MSP principles, governance themes, the transformational flow, programme information (documents) and the MSP-defined programme management roles
- Produce and evaluate examples of MSP programme information (documents).

2.2.3 Advanced Practitioner

Candidates need to exhibit the competencies required for both the Foundation and Practitioner qualifications and show that they could adapt the MSP guidance to the needs of a particular programme environment.

Candidates should be able to:

- Determine the most appropriate framework for change
- Justify specific activities that should be undertaken by each of the defined MSP roles during each of the processes of the transformational flow

- Produce, evaluate and suggest improvements to examples of MSP programme information (documents)
- Evaluate the effectiveness of the application of each of the MSP principles, the governance themes and the transformational flow processes
- Adapt the programme's approach to the governance themes to the needs of both the wider programme environment and the sponsoring organization
- Learn from experience and, as a result, propose alternative approaches that would improve the effectiveness of the application of each of the MSP principles, the governance themes and the transformational flow processes.

2.3 LEARNING OUTCOMES ASSESSMENT MODEL

2.3.1 Background

A classification widely used when designing assessments for certification and education is Bloom's *Taxonomy of Educational Objectives* (Bloom *et al.*, 1956). This classifies learning objectives into six ascending learning levels, each defining a higher degree of competency and skill.

APMG has adapted this and developed a variation of Bloom's model, the Learning Outcomes Assessment Model, which is used to define the standard for each of the APMG qualifications. The resulting qualification standards are used as a basis for classifying learning outcomes when developing the syllabus, examinations and qualification schemes for each level.

This structured approach helps to ensure that:

- There is a clear delineation in learning level content between different qualification levels

- Learning outcomes are examined consistently across different areas of the published guidance
- Examination questions and papers are consistent.

2.3.2 MSP Learning Outcomes Assessment Model

For the purpose of MSP examinations, five levels are used for classifying learning outcomes:

- Levels 1 and 2 are used for the Foundation examination

- Levels 2 to 4 are used for the Practitioner examination
- Level 5 is used for the Advanced Practitioner examination.

The tables below describe for each outcome level:

- The expectation
- How the MSP examiners have applied the APMG learning model to this level of question
- Reference to the breakdown of topics relevant to that specific area of the syllabus.

Level 1	Knowledge (information)
Generic definition from APMG's Learning Outcomes Assessment Model	Know key facts, terms and concepts from the guidance
MSP Learning Outcomes Assessment Model	Know facts, including terms, concepts, MSP principles, governance themes, transformational flow processes, and responsibilities from the guidance
Section header	Know facts, terms and concepts relating to the syllabus area Specifically to recall: [*individual lines then follow in the syllabus describing the detail required*]
Level 2	Comprehension (understanding)
Generic definition from APMG's Learning Outcomes Assessment Model	Understand concepts from the guidance
MSP Learning Outcomes Assessment Model	Understand the programme environment, MSP principles, governance themes, transformational flow processes, and responsibilities from the guidance
Section header	Understand key concepts relating to the syllabus area Specifically to identify: [*individual lines then follow in the syllabus describing the detail required*]

Table continues

Level 3	Application (using)
Generic definition from APMG's Learning Outcomes Assessment Model	Be able to apply key concepts relating to the syllabus area for a given scenario
MSP Learning Outcomes Assessment Model	Be able to: ■ Apply the MSP principles appropriately ■ Use the governance themes appropriately ■ Create the information that is required to manage a programme successfully ■ Tailor the transformational flow processes and the governance themes appropriately for a given programme scenario.
Section header	Be able to apply key concepts relating to the syllabus area within a given programme scenario. Specifically to: [*individual lines then follow in the syllabus describing the detail required*]
Level 4	Analysis (using)
Generic definition from APMG's Learning Outcomes Assessment Model	Be able to identify, analyse and distinguish between appropriate and inappropriate use of the guidance for a given scenario
MSP Learning Outcomes Assessment Model	Be able to identify, analyse and distinguish between appropriate and inappropriate use of the guidance through appraisal of completed products and planned or completed programme (and associated project) events for a given programme scenario
Section header	Be able to identify, analyse and distinguish between the appropriate and inappropriate use of key concepts relating to the syllabus area within a given programme scenario Specifically to: [*individual lines then follow in the syllabus describing the detail required*]

Level 5	Professional practice (creating and justifying)
Generic definition from APMG's Learning Outcomes Assessment Model	Not included in the four-level APMG's Learning Outcomes Assessment Model
MSP Learning Outcomes Assessment Model	Be able to develop, evaluate and propose options for tailored approaches, designs or structures and justify the value of those approaches
Section header	[*With reference to the MSP guidance, the case study and any additional information provided in the examination paper:*] Be able to propose, evaluate and justify tailored approaches to the application of key concepts relating to the syllabus area within a given programme scenario Specifically to propose, evaluate and justify: [*individual lines then follow in the syllabus describing the detail required*]

2.4 SYLLABUS AREAS

Abbreviations for syllabus areas are as follows (reflecting the order in which they appear):

Syllabus area code (appears in rationales)	Syllabus area
PT	Overview, principles and governance themes overview
OP	Organization and programme office
VS	Vision
LS	Leadership and stakeholder engagement
BM	Benefits management
BL	Blueprint design and delivery
PL	Planning and control
BC	The business case
RM	Risk and issue management
QA	Quality and assurance management
TF	Transformational flow (covering the six transformational flow processes, FA–FF)*

*See the syllabus subject area for transformational flow in section 2.6.11.

2.4.1 All syllabus areas

Questions referring to a particular syllabus area are not restricted to a particular named chapter of *Managing Successful Programmes*, e.g. Chapter 10, 'The business case'. For example, relevant business case references may be found in Chapters 1, 2, 8, 10, 14, 15, 16 and 19 together with the appendices and glossary. As a result, the scope of the business case syllabus area includes all of the guidance related to the business case contained in the MSP guide.

2.4.2 Content of boundary documents

Successful Foundation candidates should be able to identify the type of content (i.e. the programme information) that should be found in the MSP-defined boundary documents. They are not expected to be able to recall their typical contents exactly, as described in Appendix A.4 of the MSP guide.

The boundary documents are: benefit profile, benefits map, blueprint, business case, programme brief, programme definition document, programme mandate, projects dossier and vision statement. Further information on boundary documents can be found in Tables A.1 and A.2 of the MSP guide.

2.4.3 Transformational flow

It should be noted that the MSP guide states that the figure at the start of each transformational flow chapter summarizes activities, outputs, controls and roles. A candidate will be expected to understand the tasks that are necessary to complete those activities to deliver the required outputs.

2.5 SYLLABUS PRESENTATION

The APMG syllabus is structured into a number of syllabus areas. Each area is typically based upon chapters or major subject areas of the MSP guide. The subject areas are divided into topics that focus on specific detail within the required learning level for that area.

Each of the syllabus subject areas is presented in the following format:

- **Syllabus area** 'Chapter(s)' of the MSP guide
- **The learning outcomes** What candidates need to be able to do in order to demonstrate competency in that area for each level of assessment
- **Learning level** Classification of the learning level of each topic against the Learning Outcomes Assessment Model
- **Level of assessment** Foundation, Practitioner or Advanced Practitioner (as appropriate).

2.6 SYLLABUS SUMMARY

Each table in the following sections provides a summary view for the learning levels within the particular syllabus area, but without the detailed topic information that is available in the published syllabus.

For each syllabus area, the table shows:

- The syllabus area code
- The learning outcomes for each syllabus area (i.e. what candidates need to be able to do in order to demonstrate competency in that area for each level of assessment)

■ The learning levels of each learning outcome at the three practitioner levels (**F**oundation, **P**ractitioner and **A**dvanced Practitioner), graded 1–5 according to the assessment model.

The references at the end of each table relate to sample questions in later chapters of this guide.

2.6.1 Overview, principles and governance themes overview

The main chapters covering these topics in the MSP guide are Chapters 1 to 3 and Appendices A and B.

Syllabus area code: PT	Level		
	F	P	A
Know facts, terms and concepts relating to the overview, principles and governance themes overview.	1		
Understand key concepts relating to the overview, principles and governance themes overview.	2	2	
Be able to apply key concepts relating to the overview, principles and governance themes overview within a given scenario.		3	
Be able to identify, analyse and distinguish between the appropriate and inappropriate use of key concepts relating to the overview, principles and governance themes overview within a given programme scenario.		4	
[With reference to the MSP guidance, the case study and any additional information provided in the examination paper:] Be able to propose, evaluate and justify tailored approaches to the application of key concepts relating to the overview, principles and governance themes overview within a given programme scenario.			5

See sample questions:

■ PT Foundation LL1
■ PT Foundation LL2
■ PT Practitioner LL4.

2.6.2 Organization and programme office

The main chapters covering this topic in the MSP guide are Chapter 4 and Appendix C.

Syllabus area code: OP	Level		
	F	P	A
Know facts, terms and concepts relating to the governance theme organization together with programme office.	1		
Understand key concepts relating to the governance theme organization together with programme office.	2	2	
Be able to apply key concepts relating to the governance theme organization together with programme office, within a given scenario.		3	
Be able to identify, analyse and distinguish between the appropriate and inappropriate use of key concepts relating to the governance theme organization together with programme office, within a given programme scenario.		4	
[*With reference to the MSP guidance, the case study and any additional information provided in the examination paper:*] Be able to propose, evaluate and justify tailored approaches to the application of key concepts relating to the governance theme organization together with programme office, within a given programme scenario.			5

See sample questions:

- OP Foundation LL1
- OP Foundation LL2
- OP Practitioner LL3
- OP Practitioner LL4.

2.6.3 Vision

The main chapter covering this topic in the MSP guide is Chapter 5.

Syllabus area code: VS	Level		
	F	P	A
Know facts, terms and concepts relating to the governance theme vision.	1		
Understand key concepts relating to the governance theme vision.	2	2	
Be able to apply key concepts relating to the governance theme vision within a given scenario.		3	
Be able to identify, analyse and distinguish between the appropriate and inappropriate use of key concepts relating to the governance theme vision within a given scenario.		4	
[*With reference to the MSP guidance, the case study and any additional information provided in the examination paper:*] Be able to propose, evaluate and justify tailored approaches to the application of key concepts relating to the governance theme vision within a given programme scenario.			5

See sample questions:

- VS Foundation LL1
- VS Foundation LL2
- VS Practitioner LL2
- VS Practitioner LL4.

2.6.4 Leadership and stakeholder engagement

The main chapter covering this topic in the MSP guide is Chapter 6.

Syllabus area code: LS	Level		
	F	P	A
Know facts, terms and concepts relating to the governance theme leadership and stakeholder engagement.	1		
Understand key concepts relating to the governance theme leadership and stakeholder engagement.	2	2	
Be able to apply key concepts relating to the governance theme leadership and stakeholder engagement within a given scenario.		3	
Be able to identify, analyse and distinguish between the appropriate and inappropriate use of key concepts relating to the governance theme leadership and stakeholder engagement within a given scenario.		4	
[With reference to the MSP guidance, the case study and any additional information provided in the examination paper:] Be able to propose, evaluate and justify tailored approaches to the application of key concepts relating to the governance theme leadership and stakeholder engagement within a given programme scenario.			5

See sample questions:

■ LS Foundation LL1
■ LS Foundation LL2
■ LS Practitioner LL3.

2.6.5 Benefits management

The main chapter covering this topic in the MSP guide is Chapter 7.

Syllabus area code: BM	Level		
	F	P	A
Know facts, terms and concepts relating to the governance theme benefits management.	1		
Understand key concepts relating to the governance theme benefits management.	2	2	
Be able to apply key concepts relating to the governance theme benefits management within a given scenario.		3	
Be able to identify, analyse and distinguish between the appropriate and inappropriate use of key concepts relating to the governance theme benefits management within a given scenario.		4	
[With reference to the MSP guidance, the case study and any additional information provided in the examination paper:] Be able to propose, evaluate and justify tailored approaches to the application of key concepts relating to the governance theme benefits management within a given programme scenario.			5

See sample questions:

- BM Foundation LL1
- BM Foundation LL2.

2.6.6 Blueprint design and delivery

The main chapter covering this topic in the MSP guide is Chapter 8.

Syllabus area code: BL	Level		
	F	P	A
Know facts, terms and concepts relating to the governance theme blueprint design and delivery.	1		
Understand key concepts relating to the governance theme blueprint design and delivery.	2	2	
Be able to apply key concepts relating to the governance theme blueprint design and delivery within a given scenario.		3	
Be able to identify, analyse and distinguish between the appropriate and inappropriate use of key concepts relating to the governance theme blueprint design and delivery within a given scenario.		4	
[*With reference to the MSP guidance, the case study and any additional information provided in the examination paper:*] Be able to propose, evaluate and justify tailored approaches to the application of key concepts relating to the governance theme blueprint design and delivery within a given programme scenario.			5

See sample questions:

- BL Foundation LL1
- BL Foundation LL2.

2.6.7 Planning and control

The main chapter covering this topic in the MSP guide is Chapter 9.

Syllabus area code: PL	Level		
	F	P	A
Know facts, terms and concepts relating to the governance theme planning and control.	1		
Understand key concepts relating to the governance theme planning and control.	2	2	
Be able to apply key concepts relating to the governance theme planning and control within a given scenario.		3	
Be able to identify, analyse and distinguish between the appropriate and inappropriate use of key concepts relating to the governance theme planning and control within a given scenario.		4	
[With reference to the MSP guidance, the case study and any additional information provided in the examination paper:] Be able to propose, evaluate and justify tailored approaches to the application of key concepts relating to the governance theme planning and control within a given programme scenario.			5

See sample questions:

- PL Foundation LL1
- PL Foundation LL2
- PL Practitioner LL4.

2.6.8 Business case

The main chapter covering this topic in the MSP guide is Chapter 10.

Syllabus area code: BC		Level	
	F	P	A
There are no Level 1 syllabus lines for the governance theme business case.			
Understand key concepts relating to the governance theme business case.	2	2	
Be able to apply key concepts relating to the governance theme business case within a given scenario.		3	
Be able to identify, analyse and distinguish between the appropriate and inappropriate use of key concepts relating to the governance theme business case within a given scenario.		4	
[*With reference to the MSP guidance, the case study and any additional information provided in the examination paper:*] Be able to propose, evaluate and justify tailored approaches to the application of key concepts relating to the governance theme business case within a given programme scenario.			5

See sample questions:

■ BC Foundation LL2
■ BC Practitioner LL4.

2.6.9 Risk and issue management

The main chapter covering this topic in the MSP guide is Chapter 11.

Syllabus area code: RM	Level		
	F	P	A
Know facts, terms and concepts relating to the governance theme risk and issue management.	1		
Understand key concepts relating to the governance theme risk and issue management.	2	2	
Be able to apply key concepts relating to the governance theme risk and issue management within a given scenario.		3	
Be able to identify, analyse and distinguish between the appropriate and inappropriate use of key concepts relating to the governance theme risk and issue management within a given scenario.		4	
[With reference to the MSP guidance, the case study and any additional information provided in the examination paper:] Be able to propose, evaluate and justify tailored approaches to the application of key concepts relating to the governance theme risk and issue management within a given programme scenario.			5

See sample questions:

■ RM Foundation LL1
■ RM Foundation LL2.

2.6.10 Quality and assurance management

The main chapter covering this topic in the MSP guide is Chapter 12.

Syllabus area code: QA	Level		
	F	P	A
Know facts, terms and concepts relating to the governance theme quality and assurance management.	1		
Understand key concepts relating to the governance theme quality and assurance management.	2	2	
Be able to apply key concepts relating to the governance theme quality and assurance management within a given scenario.		3	
Be able to identify, analyse and distinguish between the appropriate and inappropriate use of key concepts relating to the governance theme quality and assurance management within a given scenario.		4	
[With reference to the MSP guidance, the case study and any additional information provided in the examination paper:] Be able to propose, evaluate and justify tailored approaches to the application of key concepts relating to the governance theme quality and assurance management within a given programme scenario.			5

See sample questions:

- QA Foundation LL1
- QA Foundation LL2
- QA Practitioner LL3.

2.6.11 Transformational flow

The main chapters covering this topic in the MSP guide are Chapters 13 to 19 (Part 3).

Syllabus area code: TF	Level		
	F	P	A
Know facts, terms and concepts relating to the transformational flow and its six processes.	1		
Understand key concepts relating to the transformational flow and its six processes.	2	2	
Be able to apply key concepts relating to the transformational flow and its six processes within a given scenario.		3	
Be able to identify, analyse and distinguish between the appropriate and inappropriate use of key concepts relating to the transformational flow and its six processes within a given scenario.		4	
[*With reference to the MSP guidance, the case study and any additional information provided in the examination paper:*] Be able to propose, evaluate and justify tailored approaches to the application of key concepts relating to the transformational flow and its six processes within a given programme scenario.			5

See sample questions:

- TF Foundation LL1
- TF Foundation LL2
- TF Practitioner LL3.

Note: The transformational flow syllabus area addresses the six transformational flow processes:

- Identifying a Programme (FA)
- Defining a Programme (FB)
- Managing the Tranches (FC)
- Delivering the Capability (FD)
- Realizing the Benefits (FE)
- Closing a Programme (FF).

Foundation examination

3

3 Foundation examination

3.1 PURPOSE OF THIS CHAPTER

The purpose of this chapter is to explain the format, question types and learning levels examined in the MSP Foundation examination. It gives some hints on how to tackle the examination, together with examples of questions. Associated with each question is the rationale behind the answer.

The chapter covers:

- **Examination format** This explains the examination paper structure as well as examination timings.
- **Learning levels covered** This explains the learning levels that are used in the Foundation examination.
- **Types of question** This explains what types of question are used in the MSP Foundation examination and gives examples, including hints on how to tackle each type of question.
- **Syllabus areas** This gives examples of the syllabus coverage for some of the syllabus areas, as well as sample questions showing how a particular syllabus area is examined. Hints are provided to show how each variation on each question type should be tackled.

3.2 EXAMINATION FORMAT

The Foundation examination is a one-hour multiple-choice style paper.

The examination pack issued during the examination is made up of:

- Question paper
- Answer booklet.

It is not permitted to refer to the MSP guide during the course of the Foundation examination, as this is a closed-book examination. This means that no material other than that provided with the question paper may be referred to by the candidate during the course of the examination.

In normal circumstances, papers will be marked immediately after the examination has taken place, and candidates will be informed of their provisional result by the invigilator who marked their paper. The results are reviewed by the examination board and the provisional results are normally confirmed by email within five working days of the examination.

At open-centre examinations, there may not be time to mark the paper immediately afterwards, so candidates will not receive a result until after the papers have been reviewed by the examination board.

3.3 LEARNING LEVELS COVERED

The Foundation examination asks questions at two out of the five learning levels (see Chapter 2):

- **Level 1** Knowledge
- **Level 2** Comprehension (understanding).

3.3.1 Level 1 – knowledge

This tests knowledge of the content of the MSP guide, and the questions usually use statements that are directly taken from the guide. Recall of definitions from the MSP guide and glossary would typically be tested at this level and the candidate should be familiar with them.

A typical Level 1 question might be:

What is described by the definition 'personally answerable for an activity'?

(a) Accountable

(b) Responsible

(c) Consulted

(d) Informed

This requires the candidate to 'recall/know' the definition of 'accountable'.

3.3.2 Level 2 – comprehension

Comprehension is the ability to grasp the meaning of material and interpret information in one's own words. This is the demonstration of understanding of the different ways in which MSP concepts can be described. Typically, this assesses the understanding, interpretation and use of wording which is different from the standard statements in the MSP guide, and this is a noticeable difference between Learning Level 1 and 2 questions.

This is often achieved in the examination by the question, rather than quoting directly from the text of the MSP guide, using different wording to test whether the candidate has understood the concept.

A typical Level 2 question might be:

From which perspective are risks most likely to emerge due to political influences?

(a) Programme

(b) Strategic

(c) Operational

(d) Project

Although this question could be answered by memorizing the words in the MSP guide, it can also be answered from understanding that politics, internal or external, are most likely to impact an organization at a strategic level.

Every paper meets set criteria to ensure that there is an equal proportion of each learning level in each of the sample and live papers, so there is no difference in degree of difficulty between papers. Examples of questions at each learning level will be discussed to provide a good understanding of each.

3.4 QUESTION BOOKLET

There are 75 questions – 70 examination questions and 5 trial questions – each covering a different syllabus topic. Each of the 70 questions is worth 1 mark, but the trial questions are not scored.

In common with many other examination bodies APMG uses trial questions to enable new questions to be tested without affecting candidates' marks.

The pass mark is 35/70. A candidate is expected to answer all questions. There will be no indication of which questions are examination questions and which are trials.

Foundation question answers must be recorded in the supplied answer booklet or they will not be marked. There will only ever be one answer to each question. If more than one answer is given in the answer sheet, the response line will be void and will attract no marks. Marks are not subtracted for incorrect answers.

Hints and tips

Candidates should always approach an examination using a method which suits them.

Bearing this in mind the authors of this guide have found that the following can be beneficial.

- Since there is no indication as to which are trial questions, there is no point worrying about them. Just answer all the questions on the paper!

- Go through the paper in a first non-stop 'sweep', answering all the straightforward questions to which you know the answers; ignore any long questions or those which will take longer to work out. If you have not been able to answer a question within 20 seconds leave it and move on to the next. Put a mark in the margin of the question paper against any question you do not answer on the first sweep so that you can easily find it later.

- If you do skip/miss out any questions, be particularly careful to fill in the correct lines on the answer sheets.

- Mark each answer onto the question paper first and then transfer all answers on one or two page(s) onto the answer booklet in one go – that saves a little bit of time. But do **NOT** leave filling in the answer booklet to the end. Some people run out of time and don't fill in the answer booklet and therefore get no marks!

- Look out for questions which include a negative – a **NOT** or **FALSE**. The negative word will be highlighted on the paper using bold and capital letters, but a surprising number of candidates still get the question wrong by looking for the positive rather than negative answer. Even though the word is already in bold, circle it in pencil. Highlighting the negative word will help to ensure that you recognize the negative nature of the question as you answer it.

- Beware of changing answers you have already made – general experience indicates that there are probably more changes made from correct answers to incorrect than there are from incorrect to correct! The one time an answer must be changed is where the **NOT** or **FALSE** was missed when answering the question the first time through.

- Make sure that you mark your answers clearly on the answer booklet; if you do need to make a change, however, make sure you carefully erase the previous answer.

- When you have finished, and if you have time:
  - Check that all lines in the answer booklet have one answer – and only one answer.
  - If you marked your answers on the question paper and then transferred them to the answer booklet, make sure that you have transferred the answers correctly. For example, candidates often write down A on the question paper but somehow fill in B in the answer booklet. Check this carefully.

3.5   TYPES OF QUESTION

There are a number of different test or question types used within the Foundation examination, but for each question just one of the options given as possible answers will be correct.

MSP is guidance, not a prescriptive method. It is possible that there could be other correct answers to the question in addition to the option that is given on the examination paper. What is required is to identify the one answer that is correct from the options that have been given, and not to be concerned about any other possible answers.

The test types that may be used in MSP Foundation examinations are:

■ Standard
■ Negative
■ Select.

3.5.1   Standard

What role is responsible for producing the Benefit Profiles? [*This is known as the question stem. The question stem is followed by the options below – (a) to (d) in this case.*]

(a) Business Change Manager
(b) Programme Manager
(c) Programme Office
(d) Senior Responsible Owner

Read the question carefully – it is asking for the role 'responsible for producing' so that is the question that must be answered. It is not asking who is 'accountable for them' or who 'approves them'. The correct answer is (a) Business Change Manager.

3.5.2   Negative

Which is **NOT** generally included in the Business Case? [*Notice the '**NOT**' included here in the question stem.*]

(a) Investment appraisal
(b) Timescales for achievement
(c) Detailed risk assessment
(d) Expected benefits

It is very important to recognize the **NOT** in this question. If it is read as 'Which is generally included in the Business Case?' rather than reading the whole question, the answer chosen may be the first option that is recognized as being included in the business case – and a mark is lost. The correct answer is (c) Detailed risk assessment; this should be included in the programme's risk register, whereas the business case only contains an overall risk profile.

3.5.3   Select

There are two possible styles of select question:

■ Select (list)
■ Select (evaluation).

3.5.3.1 Select (list)

During Managing the Tranches, the Programme Manager will typically be responsible for:

1   Managing risks and issues
2   Control and delivery of communications
3   Transition and stable operations
4   Procurement and contracts

(a) 1, 2, 3

(b) 1, 2, 4

(c) 1, 3, 4

(d) 2, 3, 4

To answer this question, each item in the list needs to be assessed against the question and a decision taken as to whether the programme manager is responsible for it. If the programme manager is, tick the option; if not, cross it out. Once all four options have been considered, the correct answer can be easily identified. The correct answer is (b) 1, 2, 4, as the programme manager is responsible for managing risks and issues, control and delivery of communications, and procurement and contracts.

Options (a), (c) and (d) are incorrect because each includes item (3) and the programme manager is not responsible for transition and stable operations. This is the responsibility of the business change manager(s).

3.5.3.2 Select (evaluation)

The style of this question is similar to that of the select (list) question, but it asks candidates to evaluate two statements and determine whether they are true or false.

Which of the following statements about workstreams are true?

1 Workstreams may be delineated by discipline.

2 Workstreams may be delineated by location.

(a) Only 1 is true

(b) Only 2 is true

(c) Both are true

(d) Neither is true

To answer this question, each of the two statements has to be evaluated and a decision taken as to whether it is true or false. Then the correct option can be selected from (a)–(d) as the answer. The correct answer is (c). Both 1 and 2 are true as workstreams may be delineated by discipline or location.

3.6 SYLLABUS AREAS

There are 11 syllabus areas examined as part of the MSP examinations (see section 2.4). At Foundation level each of these is examinable at Learning Levels 1 and 2 apart from the business case, which is only examinable at Level 2.

The remainder of this chapter will give examples of the types and levels of question that may be asked for each syllabus area. Cross-references in these examples are to the relevant sections in the MSP guide.

3.6.1 Overview, principles and governance themes overview (PT)

The three topics within this syllabus area are based mainly on:

- Introduction (MSP Chapter 1)
- Programme management principles (MSP Chapter 2)
- Governance themes overview (MSP Chapter 3).

However, you will also need to be familiar with Appendix A (generic text at the beginning) and Appendix B in the MSP guide.

3.6.1.1 Learning Level 1

The candidate needs to know facts, terms and concepts relating to the overview, principles and governance themes overview.

PT Foundation LL1 (example)

Topic	The three core concepts of MSP
Test objective	To recall the three core concepts of MSP
Question	Which is a core concept of the MSP framework? (a) Programme Assurance (b) Governance Themes (c) Blueprint Design and Delivery (d) Business Change Team
Rationale	(a) Incorrect. All programme management roles include a responsibility for making sure that assurance is carried out for that role's particular areas of interest (MSP section 4.12), but it is not one of the three core concepts (MSP section 1.1). (b) Correct. The MSP framework is based on three core concepts, which are the MSP Principles, Governance Themes and the Transformational Flow (MSP section 1.1). (c) Incorrect. Blueprint design and delivery is a Governance Theme within MSP (Chapter 8) but it is not one of the three core concepts (MSP section 1.1). (d) Incorrect. The Business Change Team is one of the defined roles (MSP section 4.10) but it is not one of the three core concepts (MSP section 1.1).

3.6.1.2 Learning Level 2

The candidate needs to understand key concepts relating to the overview, principles and governance themes overview. An example of a topic which is examinable is:

PT Foundation LL2

Topic	The characteristics of programmes
Test objective	To identify the characteristics of a programme
Question	Which is a characteristic of a programme?
	(a) Governance will be applied through setting organizational standards
	(b) Focus will be on management and coordination of output delivery
	(c) Governance will be implemented through governance strategies
	(d) Focus will be on the vision for the entire organization
Rationale	(a) Incorrect. Applying governance through setting organizational standards is a characteristic of a portfolio (MSP Table B.2).
	(b) Incorrect. A project focuses on management and coordination. A programme is focused on the direction and delivery of strategy (MSP Table B.2).
	(c) Correct. Programme governance is applied through programme strategies and application, complying with rather than setting organizational or portfolio standards where they exist (MSP Table B.2).
	(d) Incorrect. A portfolio focuses on the Vision and Blueprint for the entire organization (MSP Table B.2).

3.6.2 Organization and programme office (OP)

This syllabus area is based on two chapters in the MSP guide:

■ Organization (Chapter 4)
■ Programme office (Appendix C)

together with Appendix A for relevant programme documentation (A.4.12 Organization structure).

3.6.2.1 Learning Level 1

A candidate needs to know facts, terms and concepts relating to the governance theme 'programme organization' together with programme office. An example of a topic which is examinable is:

OP Foundation LL1

Topic	The two distinct roles of the programme office
Test objective	To recall the roles of the programme office
Question	Which is one of the distinct roles of a Programme Office? (a) Acting as the home for governance and control (b) Ensuring that the programme has the necessary skills (c) Briefing and liaising with the Business Change Team (d) Identifying programme dependencies
Rationale	(a) Correct. The Programme Office is the home for governance and control, including standards, approvals, financial monitoring, assurance, provision of health checks etc. (MSP section 4.11). (b) Incorrect. This is a focus of the Senior Responsible Owner, and although the Programme Office will provide advice and guidance on roles and responsibilities, it is not one of the distinct roles of the Programme Office. The two distinct roles are providing support and guidance to the projects and initiatives and, independently, acting as the home for governance and control (MSP Table 4.1 and section 4.11). (c) Incorrect. This is a focus of the Business Change Manager, and although the Programme Office will facilitate activities in the Programme Communications Plan, briefing and liaising with the Business Change Team is not one of the distinct roles of the Programme Office (MSP Table 6.5 and section 4.11). (d) Incorrect. This is a focus of the Programme Manager; the Programme Office may record information about dependencies but it is not one of its distinct roles (MSP Table 6.5 and section 4.11).

3.6.2.2 Learning Level 2

A candidate needs to understand key concepts relating to the governance theme 'programme organization' together with programme office. This means that it is important to comprehend and interpret roles and responsibilities for key roles and how the standard organization structures are set up in a programme environment. An example of a topic that is examinable is:

OP Foundation LL2

Topic	The responsibilities of the programme manager
Test objective	To identify the responsibilities of the programme manager
Question	Which is a responsibility of the Programme Manager? (a) Assuring the integrity of Benefit Profiles (b) Notifying delivery of expected benefits (c) Commissioning assurance and audit reviews (d) Managing communications with stakeholders
Rationale	(a) Incorrect. The Programme Board is responsible for assuring the integrity of Benefit Profiles (MSP section 4.7.1). (b) Incorrect. The Business Change Manager is responsible for notifying delivery of expected benefits (MSP section 4.9.1). (c) Incorrect. The Senior Responsible Owner is responsible for commissioning assurance and audit reviews (MSP section 4.6.1). (d) Correct. The Programme Manager is responsible for managing communications with stakeholders (MSP section 4.8.1).

3.6.3 Vision (VS)

This syllabus area is based on Chapter 5 in the MSP guide and Appendix A for relevant programme documentation (A.4.28 Vision statement).

3.6.3.1 Learning Level 1

A candidate needs to know facts, terms and concepts relating to the governance theme 'vision'. An example of a topic which is examinable is:

VS Foundation LL1

Topic	The definition of a vision statement
Test objective	To recall the definition of a vision statement
Question	Which is the definition of the Vision Statement of a programme? (a) A distinct change to the way an organization conducts its business (b) The scope of what a programme will cover (c) A picture of a better future (d) The totality of an organization's investment
Rationale	(a) Incorrect. A distinct change to the way an organization conducts its business is the definition of a transformation (MSP glossary). (b) Incorrect. The scope of what the programme will cover is the definition of a boundary (MSP glossary). (c) Correct. A picture of a better future that will be delivered by a programme is its Vision Statement (MSP glossary). (d) Incorrect. The totality of an organization's investment in the changes required to achieve its strategic objectives is the definition of a portfolio (MSP glossary).

3.6.3.2 Learning Level 2

A candidate needs to understand key concepts relating to the governance theme 'vision'. An example of a topic which is examinable is:

VS Foundation LL2

Topic	The areas of focus for the governance theme vision of: ■ Senior Responsible Owner ■ Programme Manager ■ Business Change Manager(s)
Test objective	Understanding who will assess the impact of the vision statement on business operations
Question	What role includes focus on reviewing any changes to business operations as a result of the Vision Statement? (a) Senior Responsible Owner (b) Business Change Manager (c) Programme Manager (d) Programme Office
Rationale	(a) Incorrect. The Senior Responsible Owner has a focus of ensuring that the organization is capable of achieving the transformation described in the Vision Statement, but it is the Business Change Manager(s) who assesses impact on business operations (MSP Table 5.1). (b) Correct. An area of focus for Business Change Managers is assessing the impact of the Vision Statement on business operations (MSP Table 5.1). (c) Incorrect. The Programme Manager has a focus on designing the delivery of capability to align with Vision Statement commitments (MSP Table 5.1). (d) Incorrect. The Programme Office focus is configuration management of the Vision Statement document (MSP Table 5.1).

3.6.4 Leadership and stakeholder engagement (LS)

This syllabus area is based on Chapter 6 of the MSP guide and Appendix A for relevant programme documentation (A.4.27 Stakeholder profiles, A.4.26 Stakeholder engagement strategy, A.4.14 Programme communications plan).

3.6.4.1 Learning Level 1

A candidate needs to know facts, terms and concepts relating to the governance theme 'leadership and stakeholder engagement'. An example of a topic which is examinable is:

LS Foundation LL1

Topic	The definition of a stakeholder
Test objective	To recall the definition of a stakeholder
Question	What is a group affected by the programme called? (a) Sponsoring Group (b) Resource Team (c) Stakeholder (d) Business Change Team
Rationale	(a) Incorrect. A Sponsor is the main driving force behind a programme (MSP glossary). (b) Incorrect. A resource is any input required by a programme (MSP section 9.2.1). (c) Correct. A Stakeholder is any individual, group or organization that can affect, be affected by, or perceives itself to be affected by a programme (MSP glossary). (d) Incorrect. A Business Change Team is a group of specialists appointed to support a Business Change Manager (MSP glossary).

3.6.4.2 Learning Level 2

A candidate needs to understand key concepts relating to the governance theme 'leadership and stakeholder engagement'. An example of a topic which is examinable is:

LS Foundation LL2

Topic	Characteristics of management and leadership
Test objective	To distinguish between management and leadership
Question	Which of the following is part of the focus of leadership?
	(a) How
	(b) When
	(c) Purpose
	(d) Process
Rationale	(a) Incorrect. The 'how' is a focus of management (MSP Table 6.1).
	(b) Incorrect. The 'when' is a focus of management (MSP Table 6.1).
	(c) Correct. The 'purpose' is a focus of leadership (MSP Table 6.1).
	(d) Incorrect. The 'process' is a focus of management (MSP Table 6.1).

3.6.5 Benefits management (BM)

This syllabus area is based on Chapter 7 of the MSP guide and Appendix A for relevant programme documentation (A.4.2 Benefits management strategy, A.4.3 Benefits map, A.4.1 Benefit profile, A.4.4 Benefits realization plan).

3.6.5.1 Learning Level 1

A candidate needs to know facts, terms and concepts relating to the governance theme 'benefits management'. An example of a topic which is examinable is:

BM Foundation LL1

Topic	The four critical validation tests of a benefit (DOAM)
Test objective	To recall the critical validation tests of a benefit (DOAM)
Question	Which are included in the critical validation tests for a benefit? 1. Description 2. Observable outputs 3. Attribution 4. Measurement (a) 1,2,3 (b) 1,2,4 (c) 1,3,4 (d) 2,3,4
Rationale	(a) Incorrect. Description and attribution are included in the critical validation tests for a benefit but a third is observable outcomes not outputs (MSP section 7.4.2.2). (b) Incorrect. Description and measurement are included in the critical validation tests for a benefit but a third is observable outcomes not outputs (MSP section 7.4.2.2). (c) Correct. Description, attribution and measurement are three of the four critical validation tests for a benefit; the fourth is observable outcomes not outputs (MSP section 7.4.2.2). (d) Incorrect. Attribution and measurement are included in the critical validation tests for a benefit but a third is observable outcomes not outputs (MSP section 7.4.2.2).

3.6.5.2 Learning Level 2

A candidate needs to understand key concepts relating to the governance theme 'benefits management'. An example of a topic which is examinable is:

BM Foundation LL2

Topic	Elements and sequencing of the path to benefit realization and corporate objectives
Test objective	To identify the sequence of the path to benefit realization
Question	Which step in the path to benefits realization and corporate objectives leads directly to the realization of further benefits?
	(a) Outcomes
	(b) Capabilities
	(c) Side-effects and consequences
	(d) Organizational changes
Rationale	(a) Incorrect. Outcomes occur after, and are enabled by, capabilities; once embedded, they will lead to realization of initial (not further) benefits (MSP Figure 7.4).
	(b) Incorrect. Capabilities occur after, and are built by, project outputs (MSP Figure 7.4).
	(c) Correct. Side-effects and consequences realize further benefits (MSP Figure 7.4).
	(d) Incorrect. Organizational changes occur after and are triggered by capabilities (MSP Figure 7.4).

3.6.6 Blueprint design and delivery (BL)

This syllabus area is based on Chapter 8 of the MSP guide and Appendix A for relevant programme documentation (A.4.5 Blueprint).

3.6.6.1 Learning Level 1

A candidate needs to know facts, terms and concepts relating to the governance theme 'blueprint design and delivery'. An example of a topic which is examinable is:

BL Foundation LL1

Topic	The definition of workstream
Test objective	To recall the definition of a workstream
Question	Which is a logical grouping of projects and activities that together enable effective management? (a) A tranche (b) A workstream (c) A programme (d) A schedule
Rationale	(a) Incorrect. A tranche is a group of projects structured around a distinct step change in capability and benefit delivery (MSP glossary). (b) Correct. A workstream is the logical grouping of projects and activities that together enable effective management (MSP glossary). (c) Incorrect. A programme is a temporary flexible organization structure created to coordinate, direct and oversee the implementation of a set of related projects and activities (MSP glossary). (d) Incorrect. A schedule provides the overall sequence and timetable for deliverables (MSP section 9.2.6).

3.6.6.2 Learning Level 2

A candidate needs to understand key concepts relating to the governance theme 'blueprint design and delivery'. An example of a topic which is examinable is:

BL Foundation LL2

Topic	The purpose and typical contents of a blueprint
Test objective	To identify the purpose of a blueprint
Question	Which is **NOT** part of the primary purpose of the Blueprint? (a) Specification of the future state (b) Communication of the future state (c) Specification of the solution set underpinning the future state (d) Ensuring coherence of the future state
Rationale	(a) Incorrect. The specification of the future state is a part of the primary purpose of the Blueprint (MSP section 8.2.1). (b) Correct. Communication of the future state is the primary purpose of the Vision Statement, not the Blueprint (MSP section 8.2.1). (c) Incorrect. Specification of the solution set underpinning the future state is a part of the primary purpose of the Blueprint (MSP section 8.2.1). (d) Incorrect. Ensuring coherence of the future state is a part of the primary purpose of the Blueprint (MSP section 8.2.1).

3.6.7 Planning and control (PL)

This syllabus area is based on Chapter 9 of the MSP guide and Appendix A for relevant programme documentation (A.4.11 Monitoring and control strategy, A.4.19 Projects dossier, A.4.17 Programme plan, A.4.23 Resource management strategy, A.4.22 Resource management plan).

3.6.7.1 Learning Level 1

A candidate needs to know facts, terms and concepts relating to the governance theme 'planning and control'. An example of a topic which is examinable is:

PL Foundation LL1

Topic	The definition of a resource
Test objective	To recall the definition of a resource
Question	What is an alternative name for any input required by a programme?
	(a) Resource
	(b) Benefit
	(c) Plan
	(d) Baseline
Rationale	(a) Correct. Any input required by a project or programme is known as a resource (MSP section 9.2.2).
	(b) Incorrect. A benefit is the measurable improvement resulting from an outcome perceived as an advantage by one or more stakeholders (MSP glossary).
	(c) Incorrect. A plan is a detailed proposal for doing or achieving something, detailing the what, when, how and by whom (MSP glossary). A plan may be an input to an activity or a process, but the question is asking for an alternative name for ANY input.
	(d) Incorrect. A baseline is a reference level against which an entity is monitored and controlled (MSP glossary).

3.6.7.2 Learning Level 2

A candidate needs to understand key concepts relating to the governance theme 'planning and control'. An example of a topic which is examinable is:

PL Foundation LL2

Topic	The ways that live projects are monitored
Test objective	To identify ways in which live projects are monitored
Question	Which is a key area on which the programme focuses when monitoring progress of projects? (a) Assurance of individual issue impact analysis (b) Creation of project briefs (c) Supplier performance (d) Intra-dependencies on other programmes
Rationale	(a) Incorrect. A programme should not micro-manage a project (MSP section 9.3). Information on issues will only be relevant at the programme level if tolerance is exceeded and exception reports are raised (MSP section 17.6). (b) Incorrect. Project briefs are developed by the programme to give each project a thorough and rapid start (MSP section 9.2.4). Therefore, these are in place prior to project development and delivery, so would not be a key focus of the monitoring of project progress. (c) Correct. Resources need to be formally managed including supplier performance (MSP section 17.6.1). (d) Incorrect. These are the dependencies that are external to an individual programme but are still within the perimeter of the organization's programme and project management environment, most likely linked to the scope of another programme or within a corporate portfolio (MSP section 9.3.2). Therefore, this is not a key area of focus for a programme monitoring the progress of its projects.

3.6.8 The business case (BC)

This syllabus area is based on Chapter 10 of the MSP guide and Appendix A for relevant programme documentation (A.4.6 Business case).

3.6.8.1 Learning Level 1

There are no Level 1 requirements relating to the business case.

3.6.8.2 Learning Level 2

A candidate needs to understand key concepts relating to the governance theme 'the business case'. An example of a topic which is examinable is:

BC Foundation LL2

Topic	The main areas of focus of the Senior Responsible Owner
Test objective	To identify main areas of focus of the Senior Responsible Owner for the governance theme 'business case'.
Question	What role is focused on ensuring that the Business Case is controlled as the programme develops? (a) Programme Manager (b) Programme Office (c) Senior Responsible Owner (d) Business Change Manager
Rationale	(a) Incorrect. The Programme Manager is focused on preparing the Business Case (MSP Table 10.2), but it is the Senior Responsible Owner who is focused on ensuring that the Business Case is controlled (MSP Table 10.2). (b) Incorrect. The Programme Office is focused on supporting the Senior Responsible Owner in compiling and updating the Business Case, but it is the Senior Responsible Owner who is focused on ensuring that the Business Case is controlled (MSP Table 10.2). (c) Correct. The Senior Responsible Owner is focused on ensuring that the Business Case is controlled (MSP Table 10.2). (d) Incorrect. The Business Change Manager is focused on ensuring that the full cost of change is being captured in the Business Case, but it is the Senior Responsible Owner who is focused on ensuring that the Business Case is controlled (MSP Table 10.2).

3.6.9 Risk and issue management (RM)

This syllabus area is based on Chapter 11 of the MSP guide (section 11.2.8 for probability impact grids, Figure 11.3 for a summary risk profile and section 11.2.11 for progress reporting) and Appendix A for relevant programme documentation (A.4.10 Issue register, A.4.9 Issue management strategy, A.4.24 Risk management strategy, A.4.25 Risk register).

3.6.9.1 Learning Level 1

A candidate needs to know facts, terms and concepts relating to the governance theme 'risk and issue management'. An example of a topic which is examinable is:

RM Foundation LL1

Topic	The definition of risk (opportunity and threat)
Test objective	To recall the definition of risk (opportunity and threat)
Question	Which is **NOT** included in the definition of risk?
	(a) An uncertain event with a favourable impact
	(b) An uncertain event with a negative impact
	(c) An unplanned event which has happened
	(d) A set of events which may have an impact on objectives
Rationale	(a) Incorrect. An uncertain event with a favourable impact is a risk (MSP section 11.1).
	(b) Incorrect. An uncertain event with a negative impact is a risk (MSP section 11.1).
	(c) Correct. An unplanned event which has happened is an issue not a risk (MSP section 11.1).
	(d) Incorrect. A set of events which may have an impact on objectives is a risk (MSP section 11.1).

3.6.9.2 Learning Level 2

A candidate needs to understand key concepts relating to the governance theme 'risk and issue management'. An example of a topic which is examinable is:

RM Foundation LL2

Topic	The descriptions of defined opportunity responses
Test objective	To identify the defined opportunity responses
Question	Which opportunity response is **BEST** associated with the expression 'implementing the cause of an opportunity'? (a) Exploit (b) Enhance (c) Transfer (d) Share
Rationale	(a) Correct. Exploit is about making the uncertain situation certain (MSP Table 11.1). (b) Incorrect. Enhance is about making the opportunity more likely to occur; it doesn't make it certain (MSP Table 11.1). (c) Incorrect. Transfer in respect of an opportunity is where a third party gains a cost benefit but the primary risk taker gains another benefit (MSP Table 11.1). (d) Incorrect. Share in respect of an opportunity is where multiple parties share the opportunity on a pain/gain basis (MSP Table 11.1).

3.6.10 Quality and assurance management (QA)

This syllabus area is based on Chapter 12 of the MSP guide and Appendix A for relevant programme documentation (A.4.21 Quality and assurance strategy, A.4.20 Quality and assurance plan, A.4.8 Information management strategy, A.4.7 Information management plan).

3.6.10.1 Learning Level 1

A candidate needs to know facts, terms and concepts relating to the governance theme 'quality and assurance management'. An example of a topic which is examinable is:

QA Foundation LL1

Topic	Techniques that may be used to help assure that the programme is being delivered optimally
Test objective	To recall techniques that may be used to help assure the programme
Question	Which check is aligned to the overall objective of a gated review? (a) Programme priorities are clearly stated (b) The programme is ready for transition (c) Conformance to standards (d) The programme is under control and on target
Rationale	(a) Incorrect. A check that the programme priorities are clearly stated is part of a Health Check (MSP Appendix D.2.1.5); although such a check may be part of a gated review, a gated review involves much more than this. (b) Incorrect. A check that a programme is ready for transition is an aspect of Realizing the Benefits (MSP section 18.2.5); although a gated review may be undertaken as part of such a check, a gated review can occur at any time. (c) Incorrect. A check that the programme is conforming to standards may be part of a gated review, but gated review involves much more than this (MSP section 12.3.2.5). (d) Correct. A gated review is an assurance control that can be planned to be undertaken at any time to check that the programme is under control and on target to meet the organization's needs. The programme is not allowed to proceed unless it has undergone the required review (MSP section 12.3.2.5).

3.6.10.2 Learning Level 2

A candidate needs to understand key concepts relating to the governance theme 'quality and assurance management'. An example of a topic which is examinable is:

QA Foundation LL2

Topic	The purpose and scope of: 1. Programme quality 2. Assurance
Test objective	To identify the purpose of assurance
Question	What describes all the systematic actions necessary to provide confidence that the target is appropriate? (a) Quality control (b) Quality management system (c) Assurance (d) Audit
Rationale	(a) Incorrect. Quality control is the process of monitoring specific results to determine whether they comply with the relevant standards (MSP glossary). (b) Incorrect. Quality management system is the complete set of quality standards, procedures and responsibilities for a site or organization (MSP glossary). (c) Correct. Assurance is all the systematic actions necessary to provide confidence that the target is appropriate (MSP glossary). (d) Incorrect. Audit is the examination of the activities of a programme with the aim of determining whether the programme is doing things correctly (MSP section 12.3.2.1).

3.6.11 The transformational flow (TF)

There are six processes and seven chapters that deal with the transformational flow in Part 3 of the MSP guide (Chapters 13 to 19). All six of the transformational flow processes are covered by a single syllabus area, but there may be multiple questions covering the six transformational flows in the examination.

3.6.11.1 Learning Level 1

A candidate needs to know facts, terms and concepts relating to the transformational flow and its six processes. An example of a topic which is examinable is:

TF Foundation LL1

Topic	The reasons for programme closure
Test objective	To recall the reasons for programme closure
Question	Which is an indicator that a programme could be a candidate for premature closure?
	(a) The Blueprint has been delivered
	(b) Changes to the external environment
	(c) The last tranche has been completed
	(d) Outcomes have been achieved
Rationale	(a) Incorrect. The Blueprint delivery is a test for planned closure, not premature closure (MSP section 19.1).
	(b) Correct. Changes to the external environment could render a programme invalid and therefore result in premature closure (MSP section 13.1).
	(c) Incorrect. The last tranche being completed is a test for planned closure, not premature closure (MSP section 19.1).
	(d) Incorrect. The outcomes being achieved is a test for planned closure, not premature closure (MSP section 19.1).

3.6.11.2 Learning Level 2

A candidate needs to understand key concepts relating to the transformational flow and its six processes. An example of a topic which is examinable is:

TF Foundation LL2

Topic	The reasons for Managing the Tranches
Test objective	To identify where an activity occurs and thus whether it is a reason for Managing the Tranches
Question	Where in the transformational flow would the activity 'maintain information and asset integrity' normally be undertaken? (a) Defining a Programme (b) Managing the Tranches (c) Delivering the Capability (d) Closing a Programme
Rationale	(a) Incorrect. Maintain information and asset integrity is not an activity in Defining the Programme (MSP Figure 15.1). (b) Correct. Maintain information and asset integrity is an activity in Managing the Tranches (MSP Figure 16.1). (c) Incorrect. Maintain information and asset integrity is not an activity in Delivering the Capability (MSP Figure 17.1). (d) Incorrect. Maintain information and asset integrity is not an activity in Closing a Programme (MSP Figure 19.1).

Practitioner examination

4 Practitioner examination

4.1 PURPOSE OF THIS CHAPTER

The purpose of this chapter is to explain the format, question types and learning levels examined in the MSP Practitioner examination. It gives examples of questions, some hints on how to tackle the examination and associated questions and the rationale behind the answer.

The chapter covers:

- **Examination format** This explains that the examination is scenario-based and explains the examination paper structure as well as examination timings.
- **Use of the MSP guide** This explains the rules relating to how the MSP guide may be used during the Practitioner examination.
- **Learning levels covered** This explains what learning levels are used in the Practitioner examination.
- **Types of question** This explains what types of question are used in the MSP Practitioner examination and gives examples, including hints on how to tackle each type of question.
- **Syllabus areas** This gives examples of the syllabus coverage for some of the syllabus areas as well as sample questions showing how a particular syllabus area is examined. Hints are provided to advise how each variation of each question type should be tackled.

4.2 EXAMINATION FORMAT

The examination is scenario-based, as the Practitioner examination requires you to apply your knowledge to a given **unseen** scenario or analyse the way that MSP has been applied. The sample paper, available from APMG, includes a scenario which is typical of the one that will be presented as part of the live examination.

The scenario used in the live examination will be seen by the candidate for the first time during the examination.

The examination pack issued during the exam is made up of:

- **Scenario booklet** This booklet is stapled in the top-left corner. The scenario finishes where it states 'End of scenario'. Additional information may be supplied for specific questions only (e.g. Question 2: Risk Management – additional information).
- **Question booklet** This booklet is stapled in the top-left corner. It consists of eight questions with multiple part-questions. Any questions which require reference to the additional information in the scenario booklet use the expression 'Using the scenario and the additional information provided for this question …').

■ **Answer booklet** This booklet is not stapled – it is a loose-leaf paper. All ovals need to be filled in carefully in pencil within the lines, and 80–100% of the oval must be filled (see section 1.6.2). Erase any answers you want to change and replace with correct ones. You are recommended not to change answers unless the previous answer was clearly wrong.

It is within the rules to take your personal copy of the MSP guide into the examination. No other materials apart from the MSP guide may be brought by the candidate into the exam room.

It is recommended that notes/comments are written in the scenario booklet and the question booklet. Highlighter pens should also be used, as required. The pages of the scenario booklet can be separated, if necessary. However, this is not recommended as pages can get lost or out of sequence!

Please note that the answer booklet should only be used to record answers, and no notes should be written on it, as this could affect the marking of the paper.

The Practitioner examination is 2½ hours' duration and has eight questions, each worth 10 marks, giving a total of 80 marks for the paper. The pass mark is 50% (40 marks).

The re-registration examination (for candidates seeking to renew their MSP Practitioner qualification after 3–5 years) is 1¼ hours long and has three questions worth 10 marks each, giving a total of 30 marks. The pass mark is 50% (15 marks).

4.2.1   Scenario booklet

The scenario will describe (paint a picture of) the organization in which the programme has been established. Typically, the scenario will be between 8,500 and 10,000 words and will include a diagram showing the timescales for the programme. Most scenarios will include headings on:

■ **Background** General scene-setting about the organization in which the programme is taking place, including reasons for the programme and information on the programme environment. This may include information on other programmes being undertaken by the sponsoring organization.

■ **Organization** Which roles have been appointed to the programme management team and who has been appointed to each role.

■ **Objectives/benefits** The strategic objectives and/or key benefits that the programme is designed to achieve. Note that in the live examination papers, this section may contain both objectives and benefits. Also, it is unlikely to specify which items are objectives and which are benefits.

■ **Stakeholders** Key stakeholders, including their view of the programme and key concerns they may have.

■ **Projects** List of projects, including their objectives and outputs as well as their dependencies – both internal and external to the programme.

■ **Timescale and tranches** The capability to be delivered by each tranche. This is accompanied by a diagram to show the timelines associated with the programme. Workstreams will be shown, where applicable.

■ **Risk and issues** A description of the major risks and issues associated with the delivery of the programme objectives.

■ **Current status** A description of what has been delivered to date (if anything), as well as any issues and any lessons learned so far.

Hints and tips

If possible, please obtain a copy of the APMG sample paper so that you can review it as you read the hints and tips.

To read the scenario efficiently it is a good idea to:

- Take about 10–15 minutes to read the scenario (definitely no more).
- Make notes in the margins about key information provided in the paragraph; for example, against the 'background' paragraph it might be appropriate to make a note 'reason' – indicating the reason for the programme. Or if an issue is identified, make a note 'issue'.
- Look at the project descriptions at a high level only – there is no need to understand dependencies at this stage. If a specific question requires this knowledge, this can be looked up at the time.
- For the timescales listed, draw these onto the timescales diagram to assist you with understanding the tranches.
- Do NOT read the additional information at this point. This should be read only when the relevant question is attempted.

4.2.1.1 Scenario facts used in examples in this chapter

Please note that the actual scenario in the live examination will have several pages. To see an example of what the actual scenario in the examination will be like, please obtain a copy of the APMG-issued sample papers. The sample papers are representative of the size and complexity of the scenario used in live papers. The example box gives a much simplified scenario for use in the sample questions in this chapter.

Scenario example: the sales channel programme

For the purposes of this chapter, a simplified scenario outline has been created with the following facts, which are used as the basis for the sample questions shown:

Background

- SalesCo: a company which has traditionally been proud of its sales-oriented culture and now has outdated sales processes, primarily handled over the phone (telesales), leading to falling sales over the past few years.

Objectives/benefits

- Deliver new sales processes through three primary channels:
  - Internet direct
  - Via 'brokers'/agents
  - Over the phone to deliver a world-class sales organization
- Deliver a cost-effective IT infrastructure
- Ensure that all members of sales staff have access to a computer to handle sales enquiries via all three sales channels
- Move to new purpose-built offices in Centralville with appropriate facilities and accommodation to meet future business needs
- Deliver increased sales through existing and new channels over the internet.

Organization

The following appointments have been made:

- Senior Responsible Owner (SRO)
- Programme Manager
- Business Change Managers (BCMs) for all areas affected by the changes.

Projects

- Project 1 (Centralville)

  This project is dependent on Project 2 (marketing strategy) which will specify marketing strategy and sales volumes from which staffing needs will be defined.
- Project 2 (marketing strategy)
- Project 3 (sales channels)

  The implementation of the new sales channels is dependent on the supply of the new computers by Project 5 (supply computers).
- Project 4 (IT network)
- Project 5 (supply computers).

Timescale and tranches diagram

See Figure 4.1 for the timeline associated with the sales channel programme.

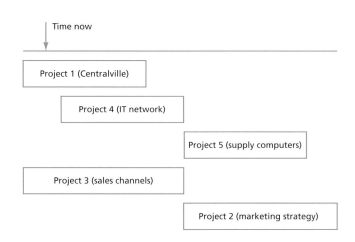

Figure 4.1 Timescale and tranches diagram for the sales channel programme

4.2.2 Question booklet

There are eight questions (worth 10 marks each) and each question will show which syllabus area is being examined at the top and the number of marks available.

Each question will be made up of part-questions, e.g. parts A, B and C. It will be clear how many marks each part-question is worth. All of the part-questions within a question will add up to 10 marks in total.

Here it can be seen that this question is about the transformational flow 'Delivering the Capability', and part A is worth 1 mark of the 10 marks in the question.

Syllabus area	Question number	Part	Marks
Transformational flow – Delivering the Capability	7	A	1

Hints and tips

To tackle the questions, it is advisable to:

- Do them in the order in which they appear. Some people try to pick and choose which questions to do first, but it is easy to miss out questions or mark answers against the wrong line in the answer booklet.

- Allow no more than 15 minutes for each full question (worth 10 marks for all part-questions). This gives 15 minutes at the end for the checking that is recommended.

- However, if you find a whole part-question confusing (e.g. you find Question 3B difficult to understand), miss it out and come back to it later when you have completed the paper. Often it becomes clear later what is required by completing other similar questions.

- If a single line is not clear, answer it to the best of your abilities, but put a question mark against the question line in the question booklet. Make a note of all the pages marked with a question mark on the front of the scenario booklet. This will give you a quick reference page to quickly find all the questions that need further review if there is time at the end.

- Do **not** leave filling in the answer booklet to the end. Some people run out of time and do not fill in the answer booklet and therefore get no marks for the examination!

- Either mark answers directly onto twhe answer booklet, or mark each answer onto the question booklet first and then transfer all answers on one page onto the answer booklet in one go. The second approach saves a little bit of time. Care needs to be

taken with both approaches to avoid filling in the wrong answer. If the second approach is used, it is advisable to check that no transcription errors have been made if there is time at the end.

- Look out for questions which include a negative – **NOT** or **FALSE**. The negative word will be highlighted on the paper by using bold and capital letters, but a surprising number of candidates still get the question wrong. They look for the positive rather than negative answer. Even though the word is already in bold, circle it in pencil; this will help to ensure that you recognize the negative nature of the question as you answer it.

- Beware of changing answers you have already made – general experience indicates that there are probably more changes made from correct answers to incorrect than there are from incorrect to correct! The one time an answer must be changed is where the **NOT** or **FALSE** was missed when answering the question the first time through.

- Make sure that you mark your answers clearly onto the answer booklet (one page at a time as stated above). If you do need to make a change, however, make sure you carefully erase the previous answer.

- Look things up, if necessary. However, be wary of trying to look up everything. Judge by the number of marks on a specific question whether it is worthwhile using the MSP guide as a reference. It is very easy to run out of time. Here are some things that can be looked up very quickly and would be worthwhile if there are at least four marks in one part-question on a single subject area:

- Appendix A documentation e.g. business case, programme plan
- Responsibilities at the end of each theme; e.g. MSP Table 8.1 gives the responsibilities for the blueprint design and delivery theme
- The RACI (Responsible, Accountable, Consulted, Informed) table at the end of each process in the transformational flow; e.g. MSP Table 17.1 gives the responsibilities for Delivering the Capability. See MSP section 13.3 for more information about RACI tables.

■ At the end of the examination, do the following checks:

- Go back to review all pages you have listed on the front cover of the scenario booklet. These are the questions where more thought was required or you wanted to use the MSP guide if there was time. Look them up or think about them again. If it is not any clearer, do not change the answer. The first answer is often right!
- Make sure that you have transferred the answers from the question booklet correctly onto the answer booklet. For example, candidates often write down A on the question booklet but somehow fill in B in the answer booklet. Check this carefully.
- Check that all lines in the answer booklet only have one answer, UNLESS it's a multiple-response type of question where more than one answer is required. (Where more than one answer is required, this will have been clearly stated in the question header.)

4.2.3 Answer booklet

The format of the answer booklet is explained in Chapter 1, section 1.6.2.

4.3 USE OF THE MSP GUIDE

The exam is 'open' book. This means that the MSP guide can be taken into the examination but nothing else. An individual's own handwritten annotations in the guide are allowed, as are stickers to mark particular pages in the books (sometimes known as 'tabs'). However, it is not permissible to stick anything in the book such as extra sheets of paper or sticky notes. The general rule is that it should be written directly onto the page in the candidate's own handwriting.

4.4 LEARNING LEVELS COVERED

The Practitioner examination asks questions at three out of the five learning levels:

- ■ **Level 2** Comprehension (understanding)
- ■ **Level 3** Application (using)
- ■ **Level 4** Analysis (using).

Every paper meets set criteria to ensure that there is an equal proportion of each learning level in each of the sample and live papers so there is no difference in degree of difficulty between papers. Examples of questions at each learning level will be presented later in this chapter to provide a good understanding of each.

For further details of the learning levels/learning outcomes examined at Practitioner level, please refer to Chapter 2, which covers the MSP syllabus.

4.5 TYPES OF QUESTION

There are a number of different test types used within the Practitioner examination. These test types are used to assess different levels of ability and are:

- Classic multiple choice
- Multiple response – note this is the only question type where more than one answer is required
- Matching
- Assertion–reason.

Every paper meets set criteria to ensure that there is an equal proportion of each question type in each of the sample and live papers, so there is no difference in degree of difficulty between papers. All of these types of question will be presented later in this chapter to provide a good understanding of each.

4.5.1.1 Information at the top of the page

In this style of question, it is important to understand what the question is asking in order to identify the correct answer. Check the information at the top of the page to find out which syllabus area the question relates to. It will be provided in the format shown below (with transformational flow – Delivering the Capability as an example).

4.5.1.2 Multiple-choice question format

Typically, there will be four options to choose from (A to D), and the question will be displayed as shown below.

Syllabus area	Question number	Part	Marks
Transformational flow – Delivering the Capability	7	A	1

Question header [*This will give general instructions about how to tackle the question.*]		
Question number [*X*]	Question stem [*This sets out the specific question.*]	
	A	[*These are the options.*]
	B	
	C	
	D	

4.5.1.3 Multiple-choice question example

Answer the following questions.		
1	Which role is responsible for aligning the costs of delivering the new IT network with the objective of cost-effective infrastructure development?	
	A	SRO
	B	Programme Manager
	C	BCM
	D	Project Manager for Project 4 (IT network upgrade)

As questions are to be answered in the context of the scenario, this is how this question should be attempted. The scenario facts include the need to develop a cost-effective infrastructure as a programme objective, and Project 4 (IT network upgrade) is included in the project list for the programme.

The question stem asks who is 'responsible' for doing a specific activity in Delivering the Capability. The answer is provided in the rationale in section 4.5.1.4. The section references quoted in the rationales refer to the relevant section of the MSP guide.

Hints and tips

It is a good idea to:

- Underline key words in the question – for example is it asking for the role which is 'accountable' or the one which is 'responsible'?
- Read each of the options carefully.
- Underline any important words in each of the options.

- Decide which options are not correct and put a cross against it/them. This will save time later and avoid having to re-read lines which have already been ruled out! For example, the SRO is unlikely to be 'responsible' for this part of the transformational flow; therefore it is possible to mark a cross against Option A immediately.

- Typically, most candidates will be able to rule out two of the options straight away (e.g. SRO and BCM). Now re-read the question stem to check that the original thoughts were correct. At this point, choose the correct answer. The RACI table can be used to look the answer up, if there's time.

- Make a note of the answer on the question booklet and then transfer the answer to the answer booklet.

4.5.1.4 Rationale

A	Incorrect	The SRO is **responsible** for leading the programme and providing overall direction for the delivery of the programme. Therefore, the SRO is **accountable** (not responsible) for aligning projects with programme objectives (MSP section 4.6.1 and Table 17.1).
B	Correct	The Programme Manager is **responsible** for ensuring that the delivery of new products meets programme requirements. Therefore, it is the Programme Manager who is **responsible** for aligning projects with programme objectives (MSP section 4.8.1 and Table 17.1).
C	Incorrect	At most, the BCM role would be consulted to assist in ensuring that the outputs meet requirements (MSP Table 17.1).
D	Incorrect	The Project Manager should deliver the scope of the project within any tolerances set by the programme (this is defined as part of the Project Brief defined by the Programme Manager). Therefore, the Project Manager is **not** responsible for aligning projects with programme objectives (MSP section 9.3.3 and Table 17.1).

4.5.2 Multiple response

Typically, there will be five options to choose from. Two answers must be chosen, and both answers must be correct to get one mark. This makes this question a little trickier than the classic multiple choice.

4.5.2.1 Multiple-response question example

Syllabus area	Question number	Part	Marks
Blueprint design and delivery	4	C	2

Points to be aware of:

■ In the final column above, 2 marks refers to the whole part-question in a paper.
■ Note that the question (below) is worth one mark.
■ Note that both answers must be correct to get one mark. The candidate needs to identify **two** answers to the same question (test objective).

Answer the following questions.

Each question provides a list of **true statements** about the programme, but only **2** statements are appropriate entries for that heading of the Blueprint.

Remember to select 2 answers to each question.

1	Which **2** statements should be included in the **final future state** section of the Blueprint under **'Processes'**?
A	Goods and services are sold via the internet direct, through 'brokers' as well as over the phone.
B	The revised sales processes will be developed by a team of sales consultants.
C	Staff will consider internet sales to be a core part of the business and will have embraced the sales processes.
D	The Business Change Team will review the number of sales per channel (internet direct, broker or phone) after completion of tranche 2.
E	25% of all sales will be through 'brokers'.

Hints and tips

It is a good idea to:

■ Follow exactly the same steps as for a classic multiple-choice question. Ruling out incorrect answers becomes even more important here, because there are now five responses to consider and reflect on!

■ Remember that both correct options must answer the question and are often facets of the same thing. Here, we are looking for two statements that are processes or business models (the way we do business around here) or are measures of operational performance.

■ The header includes a statement about **'true statements'**. The purpose of this wording is to alert the candidate to the fact that all statements in the following questions are true and do not therefore need to be verified to establish whether they are true (or not) from the scenario text. The task is to identify whether the statement is **appropriate** or **relevant**, according to MSP and the given circumstances. So in this example, all of the options are statements of what the programme is doing or will deliver. However, only two of them should be recorded in the blueprint under the **processes** heading.

4.5.2.2 Rationale

A	Correct	The sales processes and channels are part of the description of the new business model for the sales function (MSP Appendix A.4.5.2).
B	Incorrect	It is the Resource Management Strategy that provides an explanation of how resource requirements will be achieved as well as the need for subject matter experts (MSP Appendix A.4.23).
C	Incorrect	Staff opinions and attitudes towards the sales processes are part of the organizational culture or style and so should be in the organization section of the Blueprint (MSP Appendix A.4.5.2).
D	Incorrect	This describes the process and timing for a Benefits Review, which should be in the Benefits Management Strategy/Benefits Realization Plan (MSP Appendix A.4.2.2/A.4.4.2).
E	Correct	The channels through which sales are made, and the performance levels by channel, describe the business model and its performance (MSP Appendix A.4.5.2).

4.5.3 Matching

This is like a matching puzzle where you need to match the information in Column 1 to the MSP concept in Column 2. Typically, this type of question can range from 3 to 10 marks.

4.5.3.1 Matching question example

Syllabus area	Question number	Part	Marks
Transformational flow – Identifying a Programme	3	B	5

Answer the following question.

Column 1 is a list of **true statements** about the programme, which might be found in the Programme Brief. Column 2 includes a selection of Programme Brief headings. For each statement in Column 1 decide if it is an appropriate entry, and select from Column 2 the section in which it is **MOST** likely to be recorded.

Each selection from Column 2 can be used once, more than once or not at all.

Column 1	Column 2
1 Increased sales from the internet direct channel	A Should **NOT** be included in the Programme Brief
2 The number of programme staff required at headquarters in Centralville	B Outline description of benefits and significant dis-benefits
3 An increase in sales per staff member is expected	C Estimated costs and effort required
4 Floor plans for the planned Sales Team to be located at Centralville	D Risks to the programme
	E Options for delivery
5 The Chief Financial Officer is concerned that the Centralville offices might not be large enough to accommodate all staff requirements	F Assessment of the current state, the current business operation and performance in the areas impacted

Points to be aware of:

■ Notice the instruction regarding the number of times a selection from Column 2 can be used.

■ Notice the 'should NOT' included in Option A, Column 2.

Hints and tips

The purpose of this question is to match the information in Column 1 to the roles or documentation or headings in Column 2.

The best way to tackle this is to:

■ Make sure that the question is fully understood before starting to answer it. This question is worth 5 marks and it is therefore worth taking time over.

■ Read and analyse Column 2 first. If a small child were asked to sort coloured blocks of different shapes and sizes, they would not even know where to begin until they have been told how to sort – by shape, colour or size. By reading and analysing Column 2 first, it is possible for the brain to unlock what the question is asking. For example,

when reading 'outline description of benefits and significant dis-benefits', it is apparent that this would relate to an increase or reduction compared to current performance (benefits or dis-benefits).

■ Now read Column 1 and identify which item in Column 2 this relates to.

■ Note the instruction 'Each selection from Column 2 can be used once, more than once or not at all.' What this means is you could have 0 x A, 5 x B and 1 x C. The rules say that any combination is permissible. Occasionally, this instruction might change in a part-question. Do check to make sure that the standard rules apply!

■ Remember to consider what might NOT be included in the programme brief. Do this by thinking of other related documents such as the programme mandate or programme preparation plan. This will help to identify statements that should not be included in this particular document.

■ Write the answers on the question booklet
and then transfer them to the answer
booklet, page by page. Do NOT wait until
the end of the examination – you might run
out of time!

4.5.3.2 Rationale

Line number	Answer	Rationale
1	B	An increase in the sales from the internet direct channel is a benefit of the programme because it is advantageous to the company (MSP Appendix A.4.13.2).
2	C	'Programme staff' is a programme resource requirement and is included within the term 'effort' (MSP Appendix A.4.13.2).
3	B	This is an example of a benefit. The benefit is an improvement (increased sales per staff member) perceived as advantageous by the corporate stakeholder (MSP Appendix A.4.13.2 and glossary).
4	A	A description of floor plans provides detail of the building required to deliver the future state. It is the Blueprint which provides the model of the future organization and the technology that supports it (MSP section 8.2). It is the responsibility of the projects to develop more detailed designs and specifications to meet the requirements for the 'to-be' model (MSP section 15.6).
5	D	The uncertainty expressed about the suitability of the office premises in Centralville describes a risk (MSP Appendix A.4.13.2 and section 11.1).

4.5.4 Assertion–reason

This is the most complex of the question styles in use and is used to examine knowledge at Learning Level 4. These types of question test not only *what* is true but *why* it is true.

4.5.4.1 Assertion–reason question example

Syllabus area	Question number	Part	Marks
Planning and control	3	B	4

Using the scenario, answer the following question.

[*This top section, including the key to answer options, is the question header.*]

Each line in the table below consists of an assertion statement and a reason statement. For each line identify the appropriate option, from Options A to E, that applies.

Each option can be used once, more than once or not at all.

[*The next part of the question header (below) provides a key to the options used for answering the questions.*]

Option	Assertion	Reason	
A	True	True	AND the reason explains the assertion
B	True	True	BUT the reason does not explain the assertion
C	True	False	
D	False	True	
E	False	False	

Assertion			Reason
1	The specifications and design of the IT network to support the Sales Team should form part of the Programme Plan.	BECAUSE	The Programme Plan should include specifications for key project outputs.
2	The Resource Management Strategy should identify how Project 4 (IT network) and Project 5 (supply computers) will use external resources in the delivery of the new offices.	BECAUSE	The Resource Management Strategy should include the activities to monitor when resource usage by projects will take place.
3	The Programme Plan should identify a dependency between the implementation of the new sales channels and the supply of the computers.	BECAUSE	The Programme Plan should show dependencies between outputs.
4	Tight controls should be implemented for Project 2 (marketing strategy) in the Monitoring and Control Strategy.	BECAUSE	The Monitoring and Control Strategy is delivered via the Programme Plan.

A recommended procedure for tackling this type of question is as follows (see 'Hints and tips' for further advice on this):

- **Step 1** Answer **reasons** as true or false (T/F)
- **Step 2** Answer **assertions** as true or false (T/F)
- **Step 3** Look up the Cs, Ds and Es (T/F)
- **Step 4** For True/True only, choose between A and B.

Hints and tips

Although this is the most complex of questions in terms of style, it is relatively easy to master in the following way:

1 As the 'reasons' are MSP language (adapted from the MSP guidance rather than applied to the scenario) these should be answered first. To do this, cover up the assertions with your hand. Now simply put T (for True) or F (for False) against each of the reasons. Remember, the reasons can be found in the MSP guide, if there is time to look!

2 Now do the same, but for the assertions. Note that the assertions are scenario-related and are therefore applied to the scenario.

3 For all lines except the ones where we have Assertion = True; Reason = True, look up the answer on the key to answer options in the question header:

  ■ True/False = C
  ■ False/True = D
  ■ False/False = E

4 For those where you have True/True, a choice has to be made between A and B. A is where the reason explains why the assertion is true. B is where the reason does not explain why the assertion is true. It can be seen that both statements are true but are independent of each other.

Let's look at a simple example:

Assertion: The trainer is wearing a suit.
Reason: Suits are appropriate business attire.

Hopefully, it is evident that this is an A. The fact that suits are suitable business attire explains why the trainer is wearing a suit. But note the assertion is NOT that suits are the ONLY suitable business attire.

Here's a second example:

Assertion: The trainer is wearing a suit.

Reason: Trainers need to have knowledge of the subject they are training.

Hopefully, it is evident that this is a B. The fact that trainers need knowledge of the subject they are training does not explain why the trainer is wearing a suit.

So let's see how these As and Bs can be deduced in the exam:

1 Cover up the reason and consider 'why is the assertion true?' If, when the reason is revealed, it matches the reason you originally thought of, then the answer is an A. This is the simplest test, but it's robust!

2 'Reverse the order' – read the reason before the assertion: e.g. because suits are suitable business attire, the trainer is wearing a suit. This seems quite obviously an A now. Try it with the other example.

3 Look for synonyms. In the first example we have 'suit' in both the assertion and the reason and they are both the pivotal words. So there's a match. In the second example, the pivotal word in the reason is 'knowledge' and there is no reference to 'suit' at all. The only matching words are 'trainers'. Therefore this second example is a B.

4 This fourth method is the most complex test for As and Bs, but works for those who are good at mathematics: consider whether making the reason false would also make the assertion false. If this is the case, then it's an A; if not, it's a B; e.g. if a suit were not appropriate business attire, the trainer would not be wearing a suit!

4.5.4.2 Rationale

1	False: The design and specifications of the IT network to support the Sales Team is not necessary information for controlling and tracking progress and delivery of the programme and resulting outcomes. The technology to support the future organization is described in the Blueprint (MSP section 8.2). Project Briefs should include project objectives and outputs (MSP section 9.3.3).	False: The Programme Plan does not include high-level descriptions for project outputs (MSP Appendix A.4.17.2). These should be included in Project Briefs (MSP section 9.3.3).

Using the key to answers in the question header, as the assertion is false and the reason is false the answer is E.

2	True: The Resource Management Strategy should identify how the resource requirements of the programme will be achieved (MSP Appendix A.4.23.2).	False: The Resource Management Strategy is implemented by means of the Resource Management Plan which should include monitoring activities to track resource usage of projects (MSP Appendix A.4.22.2).

Using the key to answers in the question header, as the assertion is true and the reason is false the answer is C.

3	True: According to the scenario facts, the implementation of the new sales channels is dependent on the supply of the new computers. The Programme Plan should include a dependency network illustrating project input and output relationships (MSP Appendix A.4.17.2).	True: The Programme Plan should include a dependency network illustrating project input and output relationships (MSP Appendix A.4.17.2). As the Programme Plan should show a dependency network, the dependency between the outputs should be shown. Therefore the answer is A.

Using the key to answers in the question header, this is either an A or a B. As the reason **explains** why the dependency should be shown on the Programme Plan, this is clearly an A.

4	True: According to the scenario facts, there is a dependency between Project 1 (Centralville) and Project 2 (marketing strategy). Therefore, tight controls should be defined for Project 2, and these should be documented in the Monitoring and Control Strategy (MSP Appendix A.4.11.2).	True: The Programme Plan should define how the Monitoring and Control Strategy should be deployed (MSP Appendix A.4.17.2). The assertion refers to the need for tight controls and that these should be documented in the Monitoring and Control Strategy. The reason states that the Programme Plan is used as the plan to implement the Monitoring and Control Strategy. The reason (how the strategy is deployed) does not explain the need for tight controls to be documented. Therefore the answer is B.

Using the key to answers in the question header, this is either an A or a B. As the reason **does not explain** why the tight controls should be defined and documented, this is clearly a B.

There are further examples of the assertion–reason questions throughout the remainder of this chapter. In particular, there is an example of an 'A' type and a 'B' type under 'Planning and control' (see section 4.6.7 of this study guide).

4.6 SYLLABUS AREAS

There are 11 syllabus areas examined as part of the MSP Practitioner examination. Each of these is examinable at Learning Levels 2, 3 or 4 (see sections 1.4 and 2.3.2 for an explanation of learning levels). Throughout this chapter, the types of question will be illustrated as well as questions at different learning levels for a number of syllabus areas.

For further details of the syllabus areas examined at Practitioner level, please refer to section 2.6.

4.6.1 Overview, principles and governance themes overview (PT)

The three topics within this syllabus area are based mainly on the following chapters in the MSP guide:

- Introduction (Chapter 1)
- Programme management principles (Chapter 2)
- Governance themes overview (Chapter 3).

However, you will also need to be familiar with Appendix A (sections A.1–A.3, especially the generic text at the beginning), Appendix B and Appendix D as well as glossary terms.

Hints and tips

Remember, the Practitioner examination is an open-book exam so it is possible to look up the answers – if there is enough time. In many ways, looking up appropriate information can actually save time!

However, it is not advisable to try to look everything up, as it is easy to run out of time very quickly.

4.6.1.1 Learning Level 2

A candidate needs to understand key concepts relating to the overview, principles and governance themes overview. This means that a candidate needs to know the key terms and ideas and be able to recognize them in different language or when they are expressed in a different way. An example of a topic which is examinable is:

Different impacts that a change programme may be designed to deliver:

- Specification-led change
- Business transformation change
- Political and societal change.

A Learning Level 2 question requires an understanding of what it says in the guide rather than the ability to apply that knowledge and understanding. Here a candidate would need to understand that a programme that was mainly IT or engineering was a specification-led programme.

4.6.1.2 Learning Level 3

A candidate needs to apply key concepts relating to the overview, principles and governance themes overview within a given scenario.

The same areas of the book are being examined as at Learning Level 2, but this time the ability to apply knowledge to the given scenario is required. The question and options are converted to take an MSP concept and 'translate' it into scenario language. An example of how to apply knowledge is to:

- Determine (with specific reasons) the characteristics of the programme. That is, whether it may be classified as a vision-led programme, an emergent programme or a compliance programme
- Determine also the impact that the specified type of change programme has been designed to deliver.

For example: the scenario facts state that the background to the programme is 'outdated sales processes, primarily handled over the phone (telesales), leading to falling sales'.

From this statement, it can be deduced that this programme has been established by senior management to meet a particular business need. It has a specific purpose of improving sales and introducing new sales channels and is a 'top-down' or vision-led programme.

If this is compared with the example of a syllabus area at Learning Level 2, it is examining the same part of the book, but in a different way. For further details on the syllabus, please refer to section 2.6.

4.6.1.3 Learning Level 4

A candidate needs to identify, analyse and distinguish between the appropriate and inappropriate use of key concepts relating to the overview, principles and governance themes overview within a given programme scenario. This means that a candidate needs not only to be able to identify what has been applied correctly (or incorrectly), but also the reason why. Here is an example of a syllabus line at Learning Level 4 for this syllabus area:

Whether the programme has predominant characteristics of:

- A vision-led programme, an emergent programme or a compliance programme
- High, medium or low predictability
- Specification-led, business transformation or community and society.

PT Practitioner LL4

	Answer the following questions.
1	The sales channel programme has been classified as an emergent programme. Is this an appropriate application of MSP?
	A	No, because a vision-led programme is mandated to deliver a clearly defined vision.
	B	No, because a specification-led programme delivers new IT infrastructure.
	C	Yes, because an emergent programme is designed to meet a range of business needs.
	D	Yes, because an emergent programme delivers step changes in capability.

Hints and tips

For this type of question it is important to:

- Decide whether you believe the statement in the question stem to represent an appropriate application of MSP
- Once you have decided, you can then immediately review either the 'yes' or the 'no' answers, depending on your decision.

There are typically two answers to choose from (for both yes and no). It is important that the answer you choose reflects why you believe that this IS/IS NOT an appropriate application of MSP (the reason explains why it is/is not true). In other words, not only the 'yes' or 'no' has to be right BUT the statement after the 'because' also has to explain WHY it IS/IS NOT an appropriate application of MSP.

4.6.1.4 Rationale

Option	Correct/ incorrect	Rationale
A	Correct	It is not an emergent programme evolving from concurrent, individual projects that have grown within an organization (MSP section 1.6). **AND** It is a vision-led programme because it has come into existence to deliver a clearly defined vision of sales via a range of channels that has been created top down (MSP section 1.6).
B	Incorrect	It is not an emergent programme evolving from concurrent, individual projects that have grown within an organization (MSP section 1.6). It is true that a specification-led programme delivers new IT infrastructure (MSP section 1.7). **BUT** The sales channel programme is primarily a business transformation programme with a vision and desired outcomes and associated benefits (MSP section 1.7).

C	Incorrect	It is not an emergent programme evolving from concurrent, individual projects that have grown within an organization (MSP section 1.6).
		It is true that an emergent programme does emerge from a number of business needs, which is why there are many individual projects already under way in an emergent programme. However, emergent programmes then evolve into vision-led programmes to deliver a clearly defined vision (MSP section 1.6).
D	Incorrect	It is not an emergent programme evolving from concurrent, individual projects that have grown within an organization (MSP section 1.6).
		An emergent programme does deliver step changes in capability (transformational change) once it has evolved into a vision-led programme (MSP section 1.6).

Here again, if this is compared with the same syllabus area but at different learning levels, it becomes evident that there are different abilities that need to be displayed throughout the examination. Examples of questions at different learning levels will be shown in the syllabus areas that follow.

4.6.2 Organization and programme office (OP)

This syllabus area is based primarily on the following chapters in the MSP guide:

■ Organization (Chapter 4)
■ Programme office (Appendix C)
■ Appendix A for relevant programme documentation (organization structure, section A.4.12).

4.6.2.1 Learning Level 2

A candidate needs to understand key concepts relating to the governance theme 'organization' together with programme office. This means that,

for example, it is important to comprehend and interpret key attributes of the SRO, programme manager or BCM.

4.6.2.2 Learning Level 3

A candidate needs to apply key concepts relating to the governance theme organization together with programme office, within a given scenario. For example, this means that a candidate needs to be able to decide who, in a given scenario, should be appointed as SRO or programme manager. Alternatively a question could ask, in the context of the scenario, who should carry out a specific task.

Test objective

Identify candidates for the business change manager (BCM) role.

OP Practitioner LL3

Answer the following questions.		
Each question provides a list of **true statements** about the programme, but only **2** statements are appropriate when considering the appointment of the specified role.		
Remember to select 2 answers to each question.		
1	Which **2** statements should be considered when appointing BCMs to the programme?	
	A	The programme has two projects which could form an IT workstream.
	B	Project 1 (Centralville) is divided into stages that are delineated by a delivering department.
	C	The capability for tranche 2 is expected to be delivered at the end of month 15.
	D	The programme will have an impact on the sales department.
	E	The sales managers will have new responsibilities to manage staff working across three different sales channels.

Points to be aware of:

■ Notice the 'true statements' wording in the question header.

■ This is a multiple-response question, which requires 2 correct answers to get 1 mark.

Hints and tips

There is a 'true statements' wording in the question header. The purpose of this wording is to alert the candidate to the fact that all statements in the following questions are true and do not therefore need to be verified to establish whether they are true (or not) from the scenario text. The task is to identify whether the statement is APPROPRIATE or RELEVANT, according to MSP and the given circumstances.

So in analysing this question, it is true that:

A   There are two projects which could be set up as an IT workstream

B   Project 1 is divided into stages as described

C   Tranche 2 capability is due to be delivered in month 15

D   The programme is impacting on the sales department

E   Shop managers will have new responsibilities.

A decision needs to be made as to whether each of these 'facts' should be a determining factor in appointing BCMs.

BOTH answers need to answer the same test objective: in other words, both need to be factors to be considered when appointing a BCM.

4.6.2.3 Rationale

Option	Correct/ incorrect	Rationale
A	Incorrect	Although workstreams can be used to concentrate dependencies within one group or team, for example IT (MSP section 9.3.2 – Tip box), it is the business area(s) affected by the outcomes that should inform the appointment of BCMs (MSP section 4.9.2).
B	Incorrect	The fact that projects can be delineated by department (discipline) (MSP section 9.2.4) should not inform the appointment of BCMs. It should be the business area affected that influences the need for BCMs (MSP section 4.9.2).
C	Incorrect	BCMs should normally be appointed as part of Defining a Programme (MSP section 15.12), if not identified during Identifying a Programme (MSP section 14.4). The duration of the second tranche should have little effect on who to appoint or how many BCMs to appoint.
D	Correct	Each area of the business (Sponsoring Group member) that is affected by the programme should nominate its own BCM or Business Change Team representation (MSP section 4.9.2). The sales department is heavily impacted by the programme and therefore would need a BCM to be appointed.
E	Correct	The BCM should be responsible for monitoring business stability and ongoing capability to cope with the new sales processes and channels (MSP section 4.9.1) and therefore a BCM should be appointed to represent the sales department and to take on this responsibility.

4.6.2.4 Learning Level 4

A candidate needs to identify, analyse and distinguish between the appropriate and inappropriate use of key concepts relating to the governance theme organization together with programme office, within a given programme scenario. This means that you need to be able to review a statement and decide whether MSP has been applied appropriately (or not), given the circumstances in the scenario, and why.

Test objective

Identify whether a programme organization (including the appointed sponsoring group) is appropriate.

OP Practitioner LL4

Additional information for this question

[*This additional information would be contained within the scenario booklet.*]

Chief Financial Officer An experienced accountant with 10 years' experience in sales-driven organizations. Has little experience of managing programmes but is concerned that SalesCo is trying to move into too many new sales channels at once.

Using the scenario and the additional information provided for this question in the scenario booklet, answer the following questions.		
1	The Chief Financial Officer has been identified as a member of the Sponsoring Group. Is this an appropriate application of MSP for the programme?	
	A	No, because the members of the Sponsoring Group should have experience of delivering programmes.
	B	No, because the Sponsoring Group members should demonstrate their commitment to the values implied by the transformational change.
	C	Yes, because approval of programme funding needs the commitment of the Sponsoring Group.
	D	Yes, because the SRO should be an equal member of the Sponsoring Group.

Points to note:

■ This question requires you to use the additional information provided.

As the question has to be analysed in two parts, the answers in the rationale are shown in two parts to illustrate this.

Hints and tips

It is a good idea to:

- Decide whether the chief financial officer (CFO) is a suitable candidate to be a member of the sponsoring group.
- Bear in mind what it says about the CFO in the additional information. In the exam, the additional information would be found in the scenario booklet but it is shown above the question here for ease of reference.

- If the CFO is suitable, despite the lack of experience in managing programmes and projects and the doubts being displayed, review the 'yes' answers (and vice versa).
- Both the words before the 'because' and the reason after the 'because' have to be true.
- In addition, be sure that the reason (the text after the 'because') explains why the CFO should be a member of the sponsoring group.

4.6.2.5 Rationale

Option	Correct/ incorrect	Rationale
A	Incorrect	The Chief Financial Officer is a key decision-maker in relation to programme funding and should be a member of the Sponsoring Group (MSP sections 4.5 and 4.5.2). The Sponsoring Group members do not need to have programme management experience (MSP section 4.5.2).
B	Incorrect	The Chief Financial Officer is a key decision-maker in relation to programme funding and should be a member of the Sponsoring Group (MSP sections 4.5 and 4.5.2). The leaders of the programme do need to demonstrate leadership (MSP section 6.3). Although the Chief Financial Officer is concerned that SalesCo is trying to move into too many new sales channels at once, having doubts does not equate to not demonstrating the values.
C	Correct	The Chief Financial Officer is a key decision-maker in relation to programme funding and should be a member of the Sponsoring Group (MSP sections 4.5 and 4.5.2). **AND** The Sponsoring Group should authorize the programme funding (MSP section 4.5.2).
D	Incorrect	The Chief Financial Officer is a key decision-maker in relation to programme funding and should be a member of the Sponsoring Group (MSP sections 4.5 and 4.5.2). **BUT** Although it is true that the SRO is likely to be a peer member of the Sponsoring Group, this is not the reason why the Chief Financial Officer should be a member (MSP section 4.5).

4.6.3 Vision (VS)

This syllabus area is based on Chapter 5 in the MSP guide and Appendix A for relevant programme documentation (vision statement – see MSP section A.4.28).

4.6.3.1 Learning Level 2

A candidate needs to understand key concepts relating to the governance theme 'vision'. This means, for example, that a candidate needs to be able to identify transformational flow activities in relation to the development and maintenance of a vision statement.

Test objective

Understand reasons why major changes to the vision statement should be avoided.

VS Practitioner LL2

Answer the following questions about a Vision Statement.		
1		Which statement describes the reasons to avoid major changes to a Vision Statement?
	A	It was baselined at the end of Identifying a Programme.
	B	It should never be changed during the life of the programme.
	C	Changes to it may affect stakeholder perceptions of the likely success of the programme.
	D	It was agreed as part of the Programme Mandate given to the SRO.

Hints and tips

This is a typical classic-style question with nothing in particular to note.

4.6.3.2 Rationale

Option	Correct/ incorrect	Rationale
A	Incorrect	The Programme Brief, which should be created in Identifying a Programme, only contains an outline Vision Statement. This is reviewed and updated into the programme's Vision Statement during Defining a Programme (MSP sections 5.3 and 15.5).
B	Incorrect	The Vision Statement should be regarded as a constant and stable foundation for the programme once it has been approved at the end of Defining a Programme. However, making improvements to its wording or embracing newly emerged business drivers may be allowed (MSP section 5.3).
C	Correct	If the Vision Statement does require major changes, there is a risk of confusing stakeholders – possibly even undermining the credibility of the programme (MSP section 5.3).
D	Incorrect	The Vision Statement is not a heading or information to be included in the Programme Mandate given to the SRO (MSP section 14.3 and Appendix A.4).

4.6.3.3 Learning Level 3

A candidate needs to apply key concepts relating to the governance theme vision within a given scenario. Examples of the skills needed are:

■ Identify appropriate information for inclusion in the vision statement

■ Determine who should be involved in the development and (where appropriate) maintenance of the outline vision statement and vision statement throughout the life of the programme.

As an example, a candidate might need to identify statements that would be appropriate for inclusion in a vision statement for a given programme, and what would not be appropriate.

4.6.3.4 Learning Level 4

A candidate needs to identify, analyse and distinguish between the appropriate and inappropriate use of key concepts relating to the governance theme vision within a given scenario. This means that a candidate needs to be able to distinguish between what should and should not be included in a vision statement, AND why, for example.

Test objective

Analyse whether the vision statement is fit for purpose.

Additional information

[*This additional information would be contained within the scenario booklet.*]

Draft Vision Statement (may contain errors)
Training programme
Objective 1. The objective of this programme is to transform SalesCo into a world-class sales organization.
End goal of the programme When this programme is completed: 2. Sales will be generated through the three channels of internet direct, via 'brokers' and over the phone.

Points to note:

- It is stated that this document may contain errors, so some of the statements may be correct and some may be incorrect.

- The numbering here is used in the questions.

VS Practitioner LL4

Using the scenario and the additional information provided for this question in the scenario booklet, answer the following question about changes that should be made to the Vision Statement.

[*This top section, including the key to answer options, is the question header.*]

Each line in the table below consists of an assertion statement and a reason statement. For each line identify the appropriate option, from Options A to E, that applies.

Each option can be used once, more than once or not at all.

[*The next part of the question header (below) provides a key to the options used for answering the questions.*]

Option	Assertion	Reason	
A	True	True	AND the reason explains the assertion
B	True	True	BUT the reason does not explain the assertion
C	True	False	
D	False	True	
E	False	False	

Assertion		Reason	
1	No change to entry 1	BECAUSE	The Vision Statement should use language that fits the scale of change desired.
2	No change to entry 2	BECAUSE	The Vision Statement should represent the desired services and ways of working.

Hints and tips

It is advisable to:

- Firstly, read the title in the additional information. It states that the document is a draft vision statement and that it may contain errors. This means that, typically, there will be some correct statements and some incorrect ones.

- It is not necessary to read the whole piece of additional information before starting to answer the question. This is because in this question the additional information shown above is numbered. This is important, as each question line will refer to a specific numbered 'entry' in the additional information.

- Remember that in assertion–reason questions the 'reasons' should always be reviewed first to decide whether they are true or false. The 'assertions' should be covered up first and then write 'T' or 'F' against each 'reason'.

- Now answer the 'assertions' and do the same ('T' or 'F'). So in the question above, the 'assertion' states: 'No change to entry 1'. Review entry 1 in the additional information and decide whether this is an appropriate statement for a vision statement or not. If it is appropriate, choose 'true'. If it needs to be changed or removed, choose 'false'.

- It is important when answering vision statement questions in particular not to judge 'subjectively' – i.e. do not base your answer on whether the wording could be better but on whether it is an MSP-compliant statement!

4.6.3.5 Rationale

	Assertion	Reason
1	False: A Vision Statement should describe the end goal. According to the scenario facts, this is one of SalesCo's objectives rather than the end goal. A Vision Statement should not be confused with an objective, which could begin with the word 'To' (MSP section 5.2).	True: The Vision Statement should reflect the degree of transformation change in the boldness of the vision conveyed (MSP section 5.2).
	Therefore, this is a D – look at False/True in the key to the answers in the question header.	
2	True: A Vision Statement should describe the new services, improvements and innovative ways of working with stakeholders (MSP section 5.1). And, according to the scenario facts, the programme will deliver new sales channels.	True: The Vision Statement should describe new services, improvements and innovative ways of working with stakeholders (MSP section 5.1). BECAUSE the Vision Statement should describe new services or innovative ways of working, it is appropriate to describe the fact that sales will be generated through the three sales channels.
	Therefore, the answer is A.	
	There are several ways of deciding whether this second part is an A or B. The easiest method for this question is to cover up the 'reason' and decide why the Vision Statement should include the statement: 'Sales will be generated through the three channels of internet direct, via "brokers" and over the phone.'	
	The Vision Statement should include the statement because it should describe what will be new or different when the programme has delivered. This is roughly what the 'reason' states. Therefore, it is obvious that the answer is A. Other ways of determining As and Bs are shown in the hints and tips section for assertion–reason questions (see for example section 4.5.4.1).	

4.6.4 Leadership and stakeholder engagement (LS)

This syllabus area is based on Chapter 6 of the MSP guide and Appendix A for relevant programme documentation (A.4.27 Stakeholder profiles, A.4.26 Stakeholder engagement strategy, A.4.14 Programme communications plan).

4.6.4.1 Learning Level 3

A candidate needs to be able to apply key concepts relating to the governance theme leadership and stakeholder engagement within a given scenario. For example, a candidate needs to be able to identify appropriate channels of communication or messages for a given stakeholder in a specified scenario.

Test objective

Determine activities and roles involved in the development and maintenance of the documentation, throughout the life of the programme.

LS Practitioner LL3

Answer the following question.	

Column 1 is a list of key messages and programme communication activities to be carried out as part of the Programme Communications Plan. For each message in Column 1, select from Column 2 the role which should be responsible for the activities. Each selection from Column 2 can be used once, more than once or not at all. [*You can have 0 × A, 1 × A or even 6 × A.*]

Column 1	Column 2
1 Informing staff that they will be attending a 2-day training course to explain the new sales processes.	A BCM for the sales
	B BCM for IT
2 Delivering a progress statement about development of the new sales channels to members of the Corporate Board at a board meeting.	C Programme Manager
	D Project Manager for Project 5 (supply computers)
3 Presenting a formal statement to the annual shareholders' meeting on the expected date for implementing the new sales processes.	E Project Manager for Project 3 (sales channels)
	F SRO
4 Communicating with sales managers to identify additional benefits that will arise as a result of the new sales channels.	
5 Delivering regular progress reports about the progress towards delivery of the new computers.	
6 Notifying project managers within the programme about overall progress with regard to changes to job descriptions.	

Hints and tips

It is a good idea to:

- Read the question header and Column 2 first.
- It can be seen that this question relates to roles within the theme 'leadership and stakeholder engagement'. At the end of each theme there is a responsibilities table, which explains who is responsible for what, in relation to that particular theme.
- Look up the table (MSP Table 6.5); this will assist in answering the question quickly and efficiently.

4.6.4.2 Rationale

Line number	Answer	Rationale
1	A	BCMs should be responsible for engaging those operating new working practices (MSP Table 6.5). It is the BCM for the sales that would communicate this message to staff about the new sales processes that they will need to comply with.
2	F	The SRO should be responsible for leading the engagement with high-impact stakeholders, such as the Corporate Board, and anticipating stakeholder issues that may arise (MSP Table 6.5).
3	F	The SRO should engage key stakeholders early and at appropriate milestones throughout the programme and be proactive and visible as the driving force behind the programme (MSP section 4.6.2 and Table 6.5).
4	A	The BCM for the sales should be responsible for engaging with the sales managers (affected stakeholders) (MSP Table 6.5).
5	D	The Project Manager for Project 5 (supply computers) should be responsible for reporting progress on its development (MSP section 17.6.1) because projects should report in an agreed format to help aggregate the information at the programme level in line with the Monitoring and Control Strategy (MSP section 17.6.1).
6	C	The Programme Manager is responsible for controlling and aligning project communications (MSP Table 6.5).

4.6.5 Benefits management (BM)

This syllabus area is based on Chapter 7 of the MSP guide and Appendix A for relevant programme documentation (A.4.2 Benefits management strategy, A.4.3 Benefits map, A.4.1 Benefit profile, A.4.4 Benefits realization plan).

There are no sample benefits management questions included in this chapter; questions in the actual examinations may include any of the question formats used for other syllabus topics. Sample questions on this topic can be found in the APMG sample papers.

4.6.6 Blueprint design and delivery (BL)

This syllabus area is based on Chapter 8 of the MSP guide and Appendix A for relevant programme documentation (A.4.5 Blueprint).

There are no sample blueprint design and delivery questions included in this chapter; questions in the actual examinations may include any of the question formats used for other syllabus topics. Sample questions on this topic can be found in the APMG sample papers.

4.6.7 Planning and control (PL)

This syllabus area is based on Chapter 9 of the MSP guide and Appendix A for relevant programme documentation (A.4.19 Projects dossier, A.4.17 Programme plan, A.4.23 Resource management strategy, A.4.22 Resource management plan).

4.6.7.1 Learning Level 4

A candidate needs to be able to identify, analyse and distinguish between the appropriate and inappropriate use of key concepts relating to the governance theme 'planning and control' within a given scenario. For example, you will need to be able to review whether the right person was involved in making a change to the programme plan AND why they should be involved.

Test objective

Whether the programme plan and monitoring and control strategy are fit for purpose.

PL Practitioner LL4

Using the scenario, answer the following question.

[*This section, including the key to answer options, is the question header.*]

Each line in the table below consists of an assertion statement and a reason statement. For each line identify the appropriate option, from Options A to E, that applies.

Each option can be used once, more than once or not at all.

[*The next part of the question header (below) provides a key to the options used for answering the questions.*]

Option	Assertion	Reason	
A	True	True	AND the reason explains the assertion
B	True	True	BUT the reason does not explain the assertion
C	True	False	
D	False	True	
E	False	False	

Assertion			Reason	
1	The Monitoring and Control Strategy should specify whether the Project Board for Project 5 (supply computers) has the authority to authorize the contracts with the IT suppliers.	BECAUSE	The Monitoring and Control Strategy should show when audits and health checks are planned.
2	The Programme Manager should recommend that the first tranche includes a trial of the new sales processes.	BECAUSE	Early tranches may be designed as trials or pilots.
3	The Project Manager for Project 5 (supply computers) should be given clear guidelines as to when the new computers need to be ready for operational use.	BECAUSE	The boundary of the programme should define the programme scope.

Hints and tips

It is advisable to:

- Review the reason for Line 1 first. It's a good idea to think about the difference between this document and other related documents.
- For reason 2, if the answer is not immediately evident, does it align with the MSP programme management principles?
- For reason 3, what is a programme boundary – does it define the scope? This could be looked up in the MSP glossary.

- Now review the assertions.
- For Line 2 where the answer is True/True, decide whether it is an A or a B. One way of doing this is by looking for synonyms. That is, do the assertion and the reason mean the same thing in MSP terms? Does this also apply to Line 3? More ways to differentiate between As and Bs can be found in the hints and tips section for assertion–reason questions (see for example section 4.5.4.1).

4.6.7.2 Rationale

	Assertion	Reason
1	True: What controls will be in place, including project decision authority, should be stated in the Monitoring and Control Strategy. The signing of the contract with IT suppliers represents a key programme decision (Appendix A.4.11.2). The assertion refers to 'authority to authorize' which describes the 'decision authority'. If we think of the Monitoring and Control Strategy as the 'internal control strategy' then setting the decision authority would be part of the Monitoring and Control Strategy and therefore would be true.	False: It is the Quality and Assurance Plan that describes when audits and health checks are planned (Appendix A.4.20.2). The Monitoring and Control Strategy and the Quality and Assurance Strategy are very closely related. One mistake candidates often make is to confuse the two documents. The Monitoring and Control Strategy is also known as the 'internal control strategy', whereas the Quality and Assurance Strategy looks at how quality should be verified and how assurance must be undertaken. Audits and health checks are a form of assurance and therefore relate to the Quality and Assurance Strategy rather than the Monitoring and Control Strategy. Therefore this is false.
	Therefore the answer is C – as per the answer key in the question header.	

2	True: SalesCo has not tested to see whether the new sales processes will generate the sales required. Therefore, it would make sense for a project to be set up to test the validity of these assumptions (MSP section 8.3.3).	True: Early tranches may be designed as pilots or proof of concept (MSP section 8.3.3). Hence, it would make sense to commission a new project in the first tranche to test out the validity of the underlying assumptions in the programme Business Case.
		One of the MSP programme management principles is about 'remaining aligned with corporate strategy'. This principle relates to proving or disproving strategic ideas. So even if the answer was not evident, it could be deduced from this concept.

The answer is A, because they both refer to the same MSP concept – that of pilots or proof of concept. The terms are synonymous.

3	True: Projects should be given tolerances set by the programme (MSP section 9.3) and a thorough Project Brief, including how and when the project needs to escalate to the programme (MSP section 9.3.3).	True: The boundary is the scope of what a programme will cover (MSP glossary and Table A.1). The assertion is describing project tolerances relating to the timing of the new computer capability, whereas the reason is about the scope or boundary of the programme, not when it is needed. Therefore, the answer is B.
	The guidelines referred to relate to tolerances +/– for time and cost in particular. A Project Brief contains information on outputs, timescales, costs, tolerances etc. so that the Project Manager can deliver in line with the programme objectives.	A programme has its boundary defined in the Programme Mandate and the margin (the flexibility that exists) is set in the Monitoring and Control Strategy.

The answer is B, because the assertion is referring to a project-level control defined in a Project Brief, whereas the reason is referring to a programme-level control defined in the Programme Mandate. They are therefore not synonymous.

4.6.8   The business case

This syllabus area is based on Chapter 10 of the MSP guide and Appendix A for relevant programme documentation (business case – see section A.4.6).

4.6.8.1 *Learning Level 4*

A candidate needs to be able to identify, analyse and distinguish between the appropriate and inappropriate use of key concepts relating to the governance theme business case within a scenario.

For example, you will need to be able to identify whether a change to the business case (as a result of a programme event) was appropriate, or not, AND why.

Test objective

Analyse whether the business case is fit for purpose.

Additional information

[*This additional information would be contained within the scenario booklet.*]

Extract from the Draft Programme Business Case
Confirmed at the end of Defining a Programme
(All entries are **true statements** but may not be recorded under the correct heading or in the correct document.)
Section A: Strategic objectives for the programme
Centralville: office space to accommodate the new, larger sales team.

Points to note:

- It is indicated that all entries are 'true statements'.

- However, the information might be in the wrong document or under the wrong heading.

BC Practitioner LL4

Using the scenario and the additional information provided for this question in the scenario booklet, answer the following questions about the programme Business Case.		
1		Which statement applies to **Section A**?
	A	No change to entry 1 because the objectives of the programme should be included in the Business Case.
	B	Move entry 1 to the Blueprint because the Blueprint describes the buildings required for the desired future state.
	C	Move entry 1 to the Blueprint because the Blueprint describes the number of staff required for the desired future state.
	D	Amend entry 1 to include the expected increase in sales because the Business Case includes costs of delivering the programme.

Hints and tips

It is a good idea to:

- Look at the top of the additional information and see that there are 'true statements' – this means there is no need to verify them from the scenario. These can be regarded as true. **However**, the question will require a judgement to be made as to whether the information belongs in this document and/or under this heading.

- Have a quick look at the question. Line 1 refers only to entry 1 in the additional information. Therefore review entry 1 and determine whether it belongs in the business case and/or under the specified heading.

- Remember that the words before the 'because' have to be true as well as the words after the 'because'.

■ One common mistake that candidates make is to judge only on one half of the sentence and therefore select the wrong answer because of this. So some candidates choose A incorrectly because the objective described is correct, even though the statement does not belong in the business case.

4.6.8.2 Rationale

Option	Correct/ incorrect	Rationale
A	Incorrect	Although it is true that the objectives of the programme include re-designing the sales processes. **AND** The design of the Centralville office space should not be described in the Business Case (MSP Appendix A.4.6.2). This information should be included under the 'Technology' heading of the Blueprint (MSP Appendix A.4.5.2).
B	Correct	The design of the Centralville office space should be described in the Blueprint, not the Business Case (MSP Appendix A.4.5.2). **AND** The Blueprint includes a description of the buildings, included under the 'Technology' heading, required for the future business operations. This is the reason why entry 1 should be moved (Appendix A.4.5.2).
C	Incorrect	The design of the Centralville office space should be described in the Blueprint, not the Business Case (MSP Appendix A.4.5.2). **BUT** It is true that the Blueprint describes staffing levels, but entry 1 is describing the required capacity of the building (technology) not the organization structure required (MSP Appendix A.4.5.2).
D	Incorrect	The 'Strategic objectives' section of the Business Case should not include the benefits of the new sales processes – it should reflect the Vision Statement and align with the organizational context (MSP Appendix A.4.6.2). **BUT** It is true that the Business Case should include costs of delivering the programme under the expected costs and overall timescales section (MSP section 10.1 and Appendix A.4.6.2).

4.6.9 Risk and issue management (RM)

This syllabus area is based on Chapter 11 of the MSP guide (section 11.2.8 for probability impact grids, Figure 11.3 for a summary risk profile and section 11.2.11 for progress reporting) and Appendix A for relevant programme documentation (A.4.10 Issue register, A.4.9 Issue management strategy, A.4.24 Risk management strategy, A.4.25 Risk register).

There are no sample risk and issue management questions included in this chapter; questions in the actual examinations may include any of the question formats used for other syllabus topics. Sample questions on this topic can be found in the APMG sample papers.

4.6.10 Quality and assurance management (QA)

This syllabus area is based on Chapter 12 of the MSP guide and Appendix A for relevant programme documentation (A.4.21 Quality and assurance strategy, A.4.20 Quality and assurance plan, A.4.8 Information management strategy, A.4.7 Information management plan).

4.6.10.1 Learning Level 3

A candidate should be able to apply key concepts relating to the governance theme 'quality and assurance management' within a given scenario. This means that you should be able to identify quality and assurance activities that should be undertaken during a specific programme.

Test objective

A candidate must be able to determine the relationships that exist between quality and the programme management principles, together with how those principles may be tested to ensure that the programme is being delivered optimally.

QA Practitioner LL3

Using the additional information below, answer the following questions about Quality and Assurance Management.

The following area where management needs to focus to ensure the success of the programme has been agreed. The entry has been documented under 'Criteria for assessing programme success' in the Quality and Assurance Strategy.

1. All members of staff need to embrace the new sales channels and sales processes.

Remember to select 2 answers to each question.

1		Which 2 activities are **MOST** likely to contribute to achievement of the criterion described in entry 1?
	A	SRO should chair a review at the end of month 8 to check that the updated sales processes and the new sales channels have delivered the planned step change in capability.
	B	BCM for sales should chair staff briefings to present the new sales processes to affected staff and collect feedback on relevant issues raised.
	C	SRO should lead a review to verify that sales have risen as anticipated.
	D	SRO should explain the importance of all staff committing to the new sales channels to the BCMs, Programme Manager and project executives.
	E	BCM for sales should arrange user testing of the updated sales processes to support the new sales channels.

Hints and tips

In this question, the additional information is included in the question stem and relates to the relationships between quality and assurance and the programme management principles. The best place to look this up is in Chapter 12 (Quality and assurance management).

4.6.10.2 Rationale

Option	Correct/ incorrect	Rationale
A	Incorrect	It is true that the SRO should chair an end-of-tranche review to confirm that the new capability has been delivered (MSP Table 9.1). However, the updated sales processes and new sales processes would still be under development this early in the programme. In addition, the achievement of a capability will not automatically lead to delivery of the required outcome. Therefore, this is not likely to contribute to achievement of the criterion in entry 1. Transition activities are designed to achieve the embedding of the change in culture (MSP section 12.1).
B	Correct	The BCM is responsible for preparing the affected business area (sales) for transition to new ways of working (updated sales processes and new sales channels). Active stakeholder engagement is a major part of discharging this role (MSP section 4.9.1 and Table 6.5).
C	Incorrect	A benefit review would be used to verify that the benefits have been realized after implementation (MSP Table 7.3), which may be an indicator that members of staff have embraced the updated sales processes and new sales channels. However, this is not likely to contribute to achievement of the criterion in entry 1. In this case, a benefit review would gather evidence of what has been achieved to date (MSP section 7.4.4) rather than ensure delivery of entry 1.
D	Correct	The SRO chairs the Programme Board, providing clear leadership and direction. The SRO should identify and communicate the key objectives to ensure success of the programme. This should ensure that everyone is focused on those specific areas that are most important and that they are applying the programme management principles (MSP section 4.6.1 and Table 12.1).
E	Incorrect	User testing of the upgraded sales processes and new sales channel should be undertaken by Project 2 (sales channels). Testing the new sales mechanisms is not likely to contribute to the achievement of the criterion in entry 1. This would only ensure delivery of a capability and not a culture change – this would be achieved by the BCM preparing the relevant business areas for the change (MSP Table 9.1).

4.6.11 Transformational flow (TF)

The transformational flow is one syllabus area. However, there are in fact six processes and seven chapters within Part 3 of the MSP guide, covering the transformational flow (Chapters 13 to 19). As there are six processes covered by a single syllabus area, there are typically two questions set against this syllabus area.

4.6.11.1 Learning Level 3

A candidate needs to be able to apply key concepts relating to the transformational flow and its six processes within a given scenario. This might include identifying what should be included in a programme mandate or programme preparation plan, for example, or who should be involved in certain activities.

Test objective

Identify tasks that need to be undertaken in order to achieve the objectives and deliver the outputs of Delivering the Capability.

Additional information

[*This additional information would be contained within the scenario booklet for the specific question it relates to.*]

Memo about trial implementation
To: Programme Manager
From: Senior Responsible Owner
Subject: Sales channel programme: proposed trial of sales channels
I have decided that a pilot implementation is needed to test whether or not the updated sales processes and new sales channels will work.
Just one of the sales teams will have its staff trained on one of the channels and the associated sales processes. A new project to be called Project 6 (sales channel pilot) will be set up to focus on the pilot, while the other projects continue with preparations for the revision of the sales approach. This new sales team will continue to use the new sales approach throughout the programme, if the trial proves successful.
Please advise me of the process we should follow to initiate Project 6 (sales channel pilot).

Points to note:

■ This is a memo and not a numbered list. It must be read before starting the question as it introduces a change.

TF Practitioner LL3

Using the scenario and the additional information provided for this question in the scenario booklet, answer the following questions.	
1	Which activity should **NOT** occur when starting Project 6 (sales channel pilot)?
A	Ensure that the Project Manager of Project 6 understands the standards required for submission of programme information.
B	Update the Vision Statement to explain what early benefits the trial will deliver.
C	Update the Benefit Profiles to show earlier realization of increased sales to be achieved as a result of the project.
D	Update the Programme Plan to show the dependency of Project 6 on the earlier delivery of revised selected sales approach from Project 3 (sales channels).

Points to note:

- Remember that in order to answer this question successfully, it is important to read the additional information mentioned in the question header.

Hints and tips

The additional information provided is in the format of a memo. It is not numbered and therefore should be read before attempting the relevant part of the question which uses the additional information. The additional information introduces a change to the programme. It would not be possible to answer this question without knowing about this change beforehand.

4.6.11.2 Rationale

Option	Correct/ incorrect	Rationale
A	Incorrect	The requirements and configuration management standards to be applied should be notified to the Project Manager when compiling a Project Brief (MSP sections 9.3.3 and 17.2).
B	Correct	No changes to the Vision Statement should be required as it should be sufficiently flexible to encompass changes in boundaries of this nature. Furthermore, the Vision Statement should be written as 'future state' and should not show dates for benefits delivery (MSP section 5.2).
C	Incorrect	It is likely that the implementation of Project 6 (sales channel pilot) will lead to the realization of some of the benefits earlier than originally planned, and these benefits will be sustained if the trial is successful. This should therefore be reflected in the appropriate benefit profiles (MSP section 7.4.1).
D	Incorrect	It is likely that the implementation of Project 6 (sales channel pilot) will have dependencies on Project 3 (sales channels) delivering the processes and channel approach to be trialled, and these should be reflected in the Programme Plan (MSP section 9.3.2).

Advanced Practitioner examination

5

5 Advanced Practitioner examination

5.1 PURPOSE OF THIS CHAPTER

The purpose of this chapter is to explain the format, question types and learning levels examined in the MSP Advanced Practitioner examination. It gives examples of questions, some hints on how to tackle the examination and associated questions and the rationale behind the answer.

The chapter covers:

- **Examination formats** This explains the examination paper structure as well as examination timings.
- **Use of the MSP guide**
- **Learning levels covered** This explains what learning levels are used in the Advanced Practitioner examination.
- **Types of question** This explains what types of question are used in the Advanced Practitioner examination and gives examples, including hints on how to tackle each type of question.
- **Language and style** This describes the expected way in which to present answers for this style of examination.
- **Reasons why people fail** This describes common issues that cause people to fail the examination.
- **Hints and tips**
- A typical Advanced Practitioner examination part-question
- A typical Advanced Practitioner dissertation topic.

5.2 USE OF THE MSP GUIDE

This is an open-book examination. Candidates may bring into the examination the 2011 edition of the MSP guide and any other material they feel will be helpful and relevant, with the exclusion of any electronic aids.

5.3 EXAMINATION FORMATS

5.3.1 Advanced Practitioner examination

The examination is a three-hour essay-style examination, which is taken under formal examination conditions at an examination centre.

The examination is based on a complex case study, which will have been issued prior to the examination and should be used during preparation for this examination. The case study provides the background and context of the programme on which the questions are based. Where additional materials such as reports, documents, formats and diagrams are required to supplement a question, these will be provided in one or more attachments. These attachments are referred to in the question or part-question as 'exhibits'.

The examination paper consists of two or three mandatory questions, each of which is broken down into a number of part-questions. One or more exhibits provide additional information to supplement the case study.

The total number of marks available for the paper is 75. In order to pass the examination, candidates must achieve 38 marks or more. Each question and part-question is allocated a number of marks. All questions and part-questions should be answered.

Candidates are expected to derive appropriate and justified MSP-based solutions from a combination of MSP guidance, the case study and exhibits, and their own general business experience. Candidates should be able to work with and build on the information provided and to use their own general business experience to develop and express informed opinions. Candidates should use their experiences and opinions to inform the answers they give – for example, to explain how they would do things in the circumstances described. This does not mean describing candidates' own programmes and specific experiences; it means transferring and applying their knowledge and general management skills to a given set of circumstances. Candidates should not use their own experience to change the scope of the examination question.

5.3.2   Re-registration examination

For re-registration, a candidate has a choice. They can either re-sit the standard Advanced Practitioner examination, or they can choose to submit a dissertation.

The dissertation is only available as an option to candidates who already have a pass at Advanced Practitioner level and are seeking to re-register after 3–5 years.

The dissertation should be between 2,000 and 4,000 words; anything substantially outside this range is unlikely to be appropriate.

The dissertation should, if possible, cover a programme of work of which the candidate has direct experience from involvement in a programme environment within the last five years. The candidate does not need to have been the programme manager in order to write about the programme with which they were involved.

If a candidate has not worked within a programme during the last five years, they may write about the case study programme (written for the Advanced Practitioner examination) as if it were one with which they had been closely involved.

In doing so, they will need to make assumptions about how the programme progressed. These assumptions should be documented within the context section of the scenario. Any such assumptions will be accepted by the examiner as 'facts' for the purpose of the dissertation.

Preparation of the dissertation is not supervised or time-limited, and the MSP guide and any other relevant reference material may be used during its preparation.

5.4   LEARNING LEVELS COVERED

It is important to note that Advanced Practitioner examination candidates are required to focus on and demonstrate competence at Level 5, which is not assessed at either Foundation or Practitioner level.

Candidates will have been assessed extensively at Foundation level on knowledge and comprehension. At Practitioner level, candidates will have focused on application and analysis learning objectives. However all of these learning levels should also be demonstrated within answers at Advanced Practitioner.

Based on APMG's Learning Outcomes Assessment Model, the Advanced Practitioner examination therefore incorporates the learning levels examined at the Foundation and Practitioner stages:

- **Level 1** Knowledge
- **Level 2** Comprehension
- **Level 3** Application
- **Level 4** Analysis
  Plus
- **Level 5** Professional practice.
  This is the ability to develop, evaluate and propose options for tailored approaches, designs or structures, and justify the value of those approaches. The practices are based on the use of MSP in a given complex programme situation. The professional practice competence builds on the analysis competence by requiring the candidate to explain and justify opinions or recommendations that they have made.

5.5   TYPES OF QUESTION

Each question in the Advanced Practitioner examination will use a combination of the case study and any additional information provided in order to give the opportunity for the candidate to demonstrate to the examiner their knowledge and understanding of MSP and their ability to use and apply it within a complex programme scenario.

The additional information may describe a change to programme circumstances and then require candidates to demonstrate how they would apply MSP in those changed circumstances. Additionally, different questions and exhibits within the same examination paper may relate to different periods in time.

It is very important that candidates justify and explain their answers, as this is key to demonstrating competence at Learning Level 5.

The case study and the exhibits do not always describe the ideal or even appropriate use of MSP. Candidates must therefore be able to recognize and respond to errors and ambiguities. Candidates are encouraged to use their real-world general business experience as well as the case study to illustrate and justify the points that are made.

5.6   LANGUAGE AND STYLE

Candidates are **not** being examined in their good use of grammar and spelling. Answers do **not** need to be presented as essays or reports with introductions and conclusions. A paragraph structure with full sentences is **not** essential.

5.7   REASONS WHY PEOPLE FAIL

The biggest single reason why candidates fail to pass the Advanced Practitioner examination is not that they lack the necessary knowledge, understanding and experience but that they fail to demonstrate it in the answers presented: what is not written down cannot be marked.

The examiners are looking for evidence in the answers presented that the candidate has the required professional practice. MSP provides a guidance framework, not a rigid structure, and at this level the examiner is not looking for a particular correct answer – indeed for some questions there is no single right answer, what they are looking for is a demonstration of understanding of the context of the question and then a justification for the proposals, solutions and recommendations put forward.

In summary, candidates fail because they:

■ Fail to address the question asked
■ Introduce irrelevant topics
■ Include incorrect statements about MSP or the case study
■ Give answers that:
  ● Are too narrowly focused
  ● Are too general and not related to the case study
  ● Have insufficient detail for the marks available
  ● Give too much detail when making a point
  ● Contain insufficient information from the case study or exhibits to explain or justify the answer
■ Make statements without justifications
■ List information that can be found readily in the MSP guide without applying it to the case study or providing justifications for the items in the list.

It is difficult to advise **how much you should write**; it very much depends on your handwriting and writing style, but typically candidates write between 12 and 18 pages of A4. More importantly, if one part-question is worth 6 marks and another 12 marks, how much (in relative terms) is the examiner expecting you to write against each part?

What is the question asking? If a question is asking about the activities required to develop a strategy, focus on the *activities* and not the content of the strategy (using examples of content to illustrate the activities, why and how will be relevant). If a question asks *who will be involved,* consider *all* the stakeholders, not just the senior responsible owner (SRO), programme manager and business change manager (BCM).

Hints and tips

Each question and part-question is allocated a number of marks – this will be stated in the question paper.

It is a good idea to:

■ Use the number of marks available to help you plan your answers. In order to gain marks you must make justified points that allow these marks to be awarded. Each relevant point made together with its justification will probably earn one or two marks.
■ Do some planning to identify the number of points you need to make and what they should be.
■ Read your answer after you have written it, and ask yourself the question 'If I was the examiner could I find sufficient distinct points to justify the marks?'

If you are asked to make a selection or a recommendation, ensure that you make one and justify it. Part of the justification may be why other options are not appropriate – but you must make a clear justified selection if you are asked to do so.

Read the whole question first before starting to answer any individual part. Parts of questions are often related, and understanding the whole question may assist in answering the first part. For example, if part (a) of a question asks you to identify a number of stakeholders and part (b) asks you to select one and explain what their involvement in benefits realization will be, make sure you have someone appropriate in part (a) to select in part (b).

Remember, MSP, MSP, MSP! This is an MSP examination; you may write the best-ever essay on benefits realization and programme management – but if you do not relate it to MSP you will not gain many marks.

There needs to be an appropriate overall balance between:

■ MSP guidance
■ Related links to the case study and relevant exhibits, supported by:
  ● Justifications derived from the candidate's general business experience.

These three elements should be described in statements which together provide a credible and coherent explanation (see Figure 5.1).

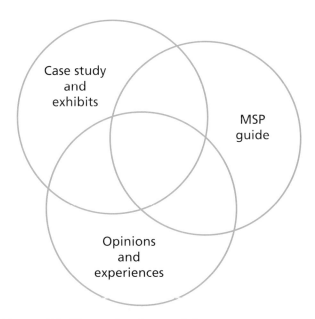

Figure 5.1 Elements of a model answer

Overall, the examination paper will require coverage of all three elements. However, this does not mean that there needs to be an equal focus on each element for each question. For example, there may be more than one case study example or justification related to any piece of MSP guidance. Candidates should use their judgement and not describe excessive case study examples against just one piece of MSP guidance or list many pieces of MSP guidance supported by only one case study example.

An answer for the whole question should reflect an appropriate balance of all three elements. There is no negative marking, but the points distribution method will ensure that a candidate will not be considered eligible for maximum marks if all three elements are not addressed. It is unlikely that a candidate will achieve more than half the marks available for an answer if it does not include any one of these elements (for example, if it does not include any valid justifications to support some MSP and case study statements).

Examiners are looking for credible answers that align with MSP. There is no single correct answer to any question, but some answers will be more credible than others. There may be several potentially conflicting answers to a question which, if appropriately explained and justified, could be deserving of equally high marks.

5.8 A TYPICAL ADVANCED PRACTITIONER EXAMINATION PART-QUESTION

5.8.1 Sample question – Stakeholders and communications (40 marks)

You are an experienced MSP consultant. Your task is to prepare materials to explain stakeholder engagement and communications in order to help inexperienced Change Team members in ABC Ltd to manage the impending change more successfully. Using Exhibit 1, answer the question below as if you were preparing notes to advise staff on this subject.

Explain and justify ways in which the information held in the Stakeholder Profiles document about each of your selected stakeholders could be used by the Change Team members in the programme. Your explanations should show how the Change Team could gain commitment from these stakeholders to the programme, and help them respond appropriately to the circumstances described in Exhibit 1.

(12 marks)

Exhibit 1

Background

The focus of the first tranche in the programme is on the formation by ABC Ltd of a partnership with XYZ Ltd. The decision to focus in this way was made because the partnership requires a significant change to the way in which the business will be run.

We are now just a few weeks away from transition in the first tranche.

Partnership negotiations have been concluded. It has been agreed that XYZ Ltd will provide specific business services for ABC Ltd. The contract is due to be signed in the next month. Administrative procedures have been amended and are ready to be implemented.

Plans have been drawn up for necessary restructuring within ABC Ltd. Some staff will transfer to XYZ Ltd. Some will remain but take on a different role. Some will take voluntary redundancy. This last group consists mainly of those close to retirement. Discussions with the staff association representing staff have been completed. The staff

(a) Select four stakeholders from Exhibit 1, one from each of the following categories:	
i.	Governance
ii.	Users/beneficiaries
iii.	Influencers
iv.	Providers

association has accepted the restructuring plans but it is clear they will scrutinize this change closely. Other staff members at ABC Ltd not directly affected by this change are worried. Some of them are not convinced that these arrangements will work and are concerned that potential future changes may lead to further redundancies.

XYZ Ltd has appointed James Kildare as its lead contact with ABC Ltd. XYZ's Chief Executive considers the partnership to be so important that James Kildare is working full-time on the relationship. Staff at XYZ Ltd are enthusiastic about the new contract. However, the Chief Executive (Charles Eggington) and James Kildare share some concerns:

- Charles Eggington was originally concerned about the lack of commercial awareness and competence of the board of ABC Ltd. While Maria de la Sancha (ABC's Procurement Manager) successfully led the partnership process and secured a good commercial deal, Charles Eggington and James Kildare remain concerned about how well the ABC managers will cope with the day-to-day running of the contract.
- Charles Eggington is still concerned about the capability and capacity of staff to manage so much change at one time.
- Charles Eggington is concerned about increasingly negative reports in the local newspaper (*The Bugle*).

5.8.2 Analysis and planning

Read the question and Exhibit 1, and analyse both.

For each part of the question:

- Check what it is asking you to do
- Consider which of the questions 'What?', 'When?', 'Who?', 'Where?', 'Why?' and 'How?' need to be addressed.

In analysing the question and Exhibit 1 there are some key points of context. You may want to consider how relevant each point is when you start to plan your answer:

- The question header provides the focus of the question – 'Stakeholders and communications'
- You are cast in the role of an experienced MSP consultant
- Through your answers to the examination questions you will help to explain stakeholder engagement and communications in the context of the programme to staff
- Note MSP elements that are mentioned which might be referenced and cross-related to each other and/or other parts of MSP:
  - Stakeholder engagement
  - Communications
  - Stakeholder profiles
- Note the new information provided:
  - Background to contract negotiations.

5.8.3 Visualization

Visualize yourself in the role of an experienced MSP consultant for the programme, in the situation described in the exhibit. Think about your own general business experience – perhaps where you have observed colleagues in a similar situation

– which might help to give you ideas about what you might do in the programme in the circumstances described.

5.8.4 Break down the question

Your answer to this question should identify four stakeholders, one from each of the listed categories, who have an interest in the programme. You should state which category each stakeholder belongs to.

You must set your answer in the context of the programme, and the stakeholders you choose must be selected from those who would have an interest in the circumstances described in Exhibit 1.

The main part of your answer to this question should focus on how stakeholder profiles for the stakeholders you have chosen from Exhibit 1 can be used to help the programme team to engage with these stakeholders. It is not enough simply to state that they are used to record stakeholders' information. Do not simply list the MSP guidance on suggested content for entries in an MSP stakeholder profiles document. Propose specific information you might record about some of these stakeholders, how this would influence usage and how the information might be used to the advantage of the programme.

There are 12 marks available for this part-question. One possible approach might be to first explain the relevance and importance of the stakeholder profiles document. You could then explain how this document might be used to support successful engagement with the selected stakeholders. Section 5.8.4.1 gives a partial answer to Q1 (a). The 0.5 in brackets indicates that this statement would gain 0.5 marks.

5.8.4.1 Partial answer to Q1 (a)

The information held in the Stakeholder Profiles indicating the relative 'importance' of stakeholders (0.5) could be shared with appropriate members of the Programme Team to aid their understanding of the current behaviours and attitudes of programme stakeholders (0.5).

Charles Eggington has concerns about lack of commercial awareness (0.5). Some members of the Programme Team may need to meet with Charles at various stages to reduce his concerns based on programme progress (0.5). The Stakeholder Profiles document should state that Charles' current position is in part due to his concerns about whether staff can perform according to the agreed contractual arrangements (0.5). Those who will engage with Charles need to be aware of the contractual arrangements (0.5). They may need to take advice on the content of the contract from Maria de la Sancha or one of her contract managers (0.5) in order to avoid a situation where their communications conflict with the terms of the contract (0.5).

5.8.5 Sample answer statements

The sample answer statements below provide examples of good, satisfactory and poor part-answers to the question. The examples also show how an examiner might mark these selected statements. Please note that these are only answer statements and not complete answers. A complete top-quality answer may comprise several similar good statements, sufficient to attract the maximum marks available.

5.8.5.1 Good answer statements for one stakeholder

XYZ Ltd as a potential future partner would be a provider (0.5).

The MSP programme could use the section in the Stakeholder Profiles document for XYZ Ltd to:

■ Record and analyse information about this stakeholder – for example, current and preferred future levels of support, interest, influence and impact (0.5)

■ Use the Stakeholder Profiles with the Business Change Team to support the cultural change process (0.5), e.g. to work/communicate in a cooperative manner, with James Kildare taking every opportunity to satisfy his concerns about the day-to-day running of the contract (0.5)

■ Brief the project teams at the start of projects about the stakeholders they will be engaging with (0.5), e.g. those who will be developing the new working arrangements between ABC and XYZ will want to know more about James Kildare as he is the lead contact (0.5).

This is a good answer statement because:

■ XYZ is a valid stakeholder from Exhibit 1. It will provide some of the means of changing the way ABC delivers services in the future.

■ The answer correctly applies MSP guidance to the purpose, use and content of the Stakeholder Profiles.

■ The answer demonstrates how the Stakeholder Profiles can be used to help guide and influence the interaction with this stakeholder in such a way that the programme is likely to be better managed.

5.8.5.2 Satisfactory answer statements

The ABC Board will want to make sure the programme delivers the strategic objectives and benefits, and should be categorized as governance (0.5).

The information held in the Stakeholder Profiles will assist in identifying how 'important' this stakeholder is to the programme (0.5) and therefore how much effort should be expended in communicating and engaging with the ABC Board (0.5). It may be used to help identify appropriate channels of communication – for example, regular programme progress presentations by the SRO at board meetings (0.5).

These are satisfactory statements because:

■ The answer starts with a correct 'governance' stakeholder and one which is relevant to Exhibit 1. However, the rest of the answer is too theoretical and is derived mainly from the MSP guide, although it is expressed in the candidate's own words.

■ It provides only one example of a specific use for the programme. While this example is relevant in the context of Exhibit 1 and in relation to particular stakeholders in Exhibit 1, it is too general. It does not explain how such communication would be used to maintain commitment or satisfy concerns. Any additional correct theoretical statements would gain no further marks.

5.8.5.3 Poor answer statements

James Kildare is in the governance category because he provides Health Solutions with account management information (0).

The Stakeholder Profiles document is used to record stakeholder information:

- Stakeholder map – stakeholders and areas of interest
- Influence/interest matrix
- Which stakeholders receive which benefits (0)

These are poor answers because:

- While James Kildare is a stakeholder, he is not in the governance category as he does not make decisions about the programme.
- The second part of the answer is information taken directly from the MSP guide. It shows no understanding of the practical use of Stakeholder Profiles and makes no attempt to contextualize the response.

5.9 A TYPICAL ADVANCED PRACTITIONER RE-REGISTRATION DISSERTATION TOPIC

When you register to submit a dissertation, you will be given a choice of four topics. Each candidate must choose one of these topics and write a 2,000- to 4,000-word essay on that topic.

A typical topic would be 'Realizing the benefits of a programme'.

The dissertation must cover the four areas:

- A brief description of the context of the programme
  (10 marks – minimum 3).
- The establishment of suitable arrangements for Realizing the Benefits given the programme context
  (20 marks – minimum 8).

- The use of MSP (either how it was used or how it could have been used) to realize the benefits
  (35 marks – minimum 20).
- Interaction with the wider organization
  (10 marks – minimum 4).

The split of marks between each area is shown. Each candidate must achieve the minimum marks shown in each area as well as the minimum overall total of 38 marks to pass.

Hints and tips

You do not have to choose a programme which used MSP. It is perfectly valid to discuss a programme that didn't use MSP, as long as you can then describe how, if MSP had been used, the programme would have been different.

You do not necessarily have to agree that the way MSP suggests something should be done would have been the most appropriate way of doing it on the programme being discussed. Provided you justify why a different approach to that suggested in MSP was, or would have been, appropriate then available marks will be awarded.

5.9.1 Context

Since you will normally be writing about a real-life programme you have worked on, the examiner will only know how big it was, the type of organization, timescales and your role from what you have written in your dissertation.

These are easy marks; there is no right or wrong. Marks are awarded purely on the basis that you have described the context of an appropriate programme.

5.9.2 Explain how and why the arrangements were set up

For the example topic given, how were the arrangements for Realizing the Benefits set up for the programme being discussed and how do these arrangements relate (positively or negatively) to the model set out in MSP guidance?

A statement that Realizing the Benefits was set up in accordance with MSP principles will not gain many marks.

An explanation along the following lines would be appropriate: how the MSP key roles (or their equivalents) were engaged in the context of realizing benefits and the specific programme, and why they needed to be engaged.

5.9.3 The use of MSP

This is the core of the dissertation:

- How MSP was used or how it could have been used.
- How MSP was implemented and where the strengths (and weaknesses) of this implementation lie.

- How MSP dealt with the relevant issues that arose during the programme's life-span, or an appreciation of how MSP would have assisted the programme's running in the chosen area had it been implemented.

For the example topic given above:

- Was Realizing the Benefits successful?
- What were the reasons for it being successful?
- How would the use of MSP guidance in this area have assisted?

5.9.4 Interaction with the wider organization

Brief summary of how the use of MSP in this area affected:

- Other areas within the same programme
- Other programmes **and/or** the wider organizational use of MSP
- A brief summary and conclusion to include any lessons learned about the use of MSP for the option chosen.

Revision guide

6

6   Revision guide

This chapter sets out some strategies for revising when preparing for all levels of MSP examinations.

6.1   FOUNDATION LEVEL

As described elsewhere the Foundation examination is designed to test Level 1 (knowledge) and Level 2 (understanding). To be successful, therefore, it is important to recognize key terms and have an understanding of how they are used in MSP.

It is not necessary, however, to learn by rote every table and diagram in the MSP guide. Because of the nature of an objective test examination (OTE) multiple-choice examination, you don't have to remember and be able to write down the names of lists of documents, themes, processes etc. What you do need to be able to do is to recognize them when they appear on the question paper.

So, for example, you are expected to recognize all the names of the key 'information sources' or 'documents' that appear in MSP. You are expected to understand their purpose. That is more than just being able to write down the words that appear under the purpose headings in Appendix A.

In order to understand the purpose of a document you will need to have a broad understanding of its content and why that content is there. Again, the emphasis is not on knowing the headings by rote. It is about having a broader view such as the fact that a benefit profile will include information about the business changes that are required.

Without this information, it is not possible to understand what the costs will be or how measurements will be made.

In order to assist your revision a number of worksheets are provided. You can use these to track your knowledge and understanding of documents, roles etc.

6.2   PRACTITIONER LEVEL

As described elsewhere, the Practitioner examination is designed to test Level 2 (understanding), Level 3 (application) and Level 4 (analysis). Even though the examination is not directly designed to test recall, the knowledge gained at Foundation level is necessary to be able to pass the Practitioner examination. If you are not taking the Practitioner examination immediately after sitting the Foundation examination (or are taking a Practitioner re-registration) it is advisable to revise the Foundation material.

The Practitioner examination is 'open book' and you are allowed to use an MSP guide during the examination, but it is unlikely that a candidate will have the time to look up every answer in the MSP guide. As described in Chapter 4 of this study guide, handwritten annotations to the guide and the addition of index tabs are permissible (see section 4.3).

When revising it is important to familiarize yourself with the structure of the MSP guide and to add appropriate notes and tabs so that, during the examination, time is not wasted trying to find a relevant reference.

6.3 ADVANCED PRACTITIONER LEVEL

The Advanced Practitioner examination is a very different style of examination to the Foundation and Practitioner tests. It is a three-hour handwritten essay-based examination. The majority of people taking the examination will, in working life, normally use computers and will therefore be unused to writing by hand for this length of time.

When preparing a paper using a computer, it is common to get the ideas down and then reorganize them later. This isn't appropriate when writing by hand; some planning before starting to write is generally a good idea, and it is useful to practise this during the revision process.

A candidate who does not often write in longhand may find it helpful to practise their handwriting. Is it going to be legible? No one would run a marathon without any training!

The Advanced Practitioner examination requires answers that illustrate the ability to relate the various aspects of MSP guidance, together with the justification for doing things at the appropriate time.

A useful revision approach is, therefore, to consider each MSP information source/document and think through:

- What is its purpose?
- Why is it produced?
- At what point in time is it produced?
- Why is it created/revised when it is?
- What will be the impact of an inadequate document later in the programme?
- The chain of events that follow. As an example, an inappropriate vision statement will lead to the following problems:
  - The blueprint will fail to adequately describe the desired future state.
  - The business case will not have captured the true costs and benefits.
  - The correct stakeholders may not be engaged.
  - The benefit profiles will be incomplete.
  - There will be a failure to realize the appropriate benefits.

Following similar thought processes through in respect to other aspects of MSP documents, roles, themes etc. will equip the Advanced Practitioner candidate with a firm grasp of the ways in which components of MSP interconnect. The candidate will need to demonstrate an understanding of these interconnecting concepts in order to pass the Advanced Practitioner examination.

The answers provided during the examination will then demonstrate the required comprehensive understanding of MSP guidance and how it can be appropriately used within a particular programme context.

6.4 WORKSHEETS

Use these worksheets as a guide to revision, filling in the columns as you cover each aspect.

6.4.1 Information sources and documents

Title	Purpose	Information baseline	In which process it is created
Benefit profile			
Benefits management strategy			
Benefits map			
Benefits realization plan			
Blueprint			
Business case			
Information management plan			
Information management strategy			
Issue management strategy			
Issue register			
Monitoring and control strategy			
Organization structure			
Programme brief			
Programme communications plan			
Programme definition document			
Programme mandate			
Programme plan			
Programme preparation plan			
Projects dossier			
Quality and assurance plan			
Quality and assurance strategy			

Table continues

Title	Purpose	Information baseline	In which process it is created
Resource management plan			
Resource management strategy			
Risk management strategy			
Risk register			
Stakeholder engagement strategy			
Stakeholder profiles			
Vision statement			

6.4.2 Inputs and outputs

Process within the transformation flow	Inputs	Outputs
Identifying a Programme		
Defining a Programme		
Managing the Tranches		
Delivering the Capability		
Realizing the Benefits		
Closing a Programme		

6.4.3 Syllabus area – responsibilities and accountabilities

Theme	SRO	Programme manager	BCM	Programme office
Organization and programme office				
Vision				
Leadership and stakeholder engagement				
Benefits management				
Blueprint design and delivery				
Planning and control				
Business case				
Risk and issue management				
Quality and assurance management				

6.4.4 Key definitions

This table should be used to revise as many terms as possible. It is particularly useful to use it for terms that are not so familiar. It can be added to, as required.

Term	Definition
Assurance	
Benefit	
Boundary	
Business change team	
Capability	
Configuration management	
Dis-benefit	
Governance	
Outcome	
Output	
Portfolio	
Programme	
Programme management	
Project	
Tolerance	
Transition	
Workstream	

Appendix A: Structure
of the MSP guide

Appendix A: Structure of the MSP guide

A.1 PURPOSE OF THIS APPENDIX

The purpose of this appendix is to provide an overview of the structure/format of the MSP guide. This appendix covers:

- MSP guide format
  - **Part 1** Introduction and programme management principles
  - **Part 2** Governance themes
  - **Part 3** Transformational flow
  - **Part 4** Appendices.

A.2 MSP GUIDE FORMAT

The MSP guide is split into four main parts, with the first three parts covering the three core concepts on which MSP is based:

- MSP principles
- MSP governance themes
- MSP transformational flow.

The final part of the guide contains the associated appendices, giving guidance on a range of subjects such as the content of MSP information (documents), how to adopt MSP as an organizational standard, the role of a programme office and health checks.

Part 1 Introduction and programme management principles

This part of the guide is made up of two chapters covering:

- Introduction
- Programme management principles.

Introduction

This chapter of the MSP guide provides an overview of what programme management is and when it should be applied. It explains how programmes come about and the characteristics of different types of programme.

Programme management principles

This chapter of the MSP guide explains the seven principles that reflect the characteristics of successful programmes. Principles are derived from lessons learned in programmes that had both positive and negative results. They represent the common factors that underpin the success of any programme of transformational change.

Part 2 Governance themes

The first chapter in this part of the MSP guide is 'Governance themes overview', which explains the nature of governance and how it is implemented in MSP.

Part 2 then continues with individual chapters on each of the governance themes:

- Organization
- Vision
- Leadership and stakeholder engagement
- Benefits management
- Blueprint design and delivery

- Planning and control
- Business case
- Risk and issue management
- Quality and assurance management.

Each of the theme chapters (excluding 'Governance themes overview') has a common structure:

- **Introduction** Establishing a clear purpose for the particular theme
- **Theme-specific information** Such as the nature or characteristics of the particular governance theme
- **Interaction of the theme within the transformational flow** Giving guidance as to how the theme should be applied throughout the implementation of the MSP transformational flow
- **Key roles** Specific guidance on which role should undertake the activities associated with the specific theme, shown in a table.

Part 3 Transformational flow

The first chapter in this part of the MSP guide is 'Transformational flow overview', which explains the nature of the transformational flow and how it is implemented in MSP.

Part 3 continues with individual chapters on each process within the transformational flow:

- Identifying a Programme
- Defining a Programme
- Managing the Tranches
- Delivering the Capability
- Realizing the Benefits
- Closing a Programme

Each of the transformational flow chapters (excluding 'Transformational flow overview') has a common structure:

- **Introduction** Providing an overview and purpose to the particular process within the transformational flow
- **Overview diagram** Showing the inputs/ outputs, principal controls and key roles as well as the activities (in the blue box) within the transformational flow
- **Activities** Details of each of the activities which are recommended in this part of the transformational flow
- **Responsibilities table** Showing who should be responsible, accountable, consulted or informed as part of the transformational flow activities.

Part 4 Appendices

This part of the MSP guide is made up of four appendices, further information and a glossary:

- **Appendix A: Programme information** Guidance as to typical contents for programme documentation, who should be involved in its production and when it should be created
- **Appendix B: Adopting MSP** Guidance on what brings about the need for programme management, how to assess organizational readiness using P3M3 and how MSP may be embedded in an organization
- **Appendix C: Programme office** Providing advice on how a programme office can assist in successful programme delivery
- **Appendix D: Health checks** Providing an overview of this quality tool and how it can be implemented
- **Further information** A list of useful references, some of which were used in the MSP guide
- **Glossary** A glossary of key MSP and Best Management Practice terms.

Further information

Further information

READING

Bloom, B. S., Engelhart, M. D., Furst, E. J.,
Hill, W. H. & Krathwohl, D. R. (1956). *Taxonomy
of Educational Objectives: The Classification of
Educational Goals. Handbook I: Cognitive Domain.*
Longmans, New York.

Cabinet Office (2011). *Managing Successful
Programmes.* The Stationery Office, London.

The following three sets of guidance are published
by APMG:

*MSP Foundation Exam Candidate Guidance
Version 1.1*

*MSP Practitioner Exam Candidate Guidance
Version 1.1*

*MSP Advanced Practitioner Exam Candidate
Guidance Version 1.1*

WEBSITES

APMG-International

Information about the examinations, accredited
trainers and consultants can be found at:

www.apmg-international.com

Best Management Practice

Provides information about all Best Management
Practice guidance, news and events:

www.best-management-practice.com

Cabinet Office

The home website for the government department
responsible for Best Management Practice:

www.cabinetoffice.gov.uk

Glossary

Glossary

accountable

Personally answerable for an activity. Accountability cannot be delegated, unlike responsibility.

as-is state

The current operating structure and performance of the parts of the business which will be impacted by a programme.

assurance

All the systematic actions necessary to provide confidence that the target (system, process, organization, programme, project, outcome, benefit, capability, product output, deliverable) is appropriate. Appropriateness might be defined subjectively or objectively in different circumstances. The implication is that assurance will have a level of independence from that which is being assured.

baseline

A reference level against which an entity is monitored and controlled.

benefit

The measurable improvement resulting from an outcome perceived as an advantage by one or more stakeholders, and which contributes towards one or more organizational objective(s).

benefits management

The identification, definition, tracking, realization and optimization of benefits within and beyond a programme.

benefits register

Summary document that contains key information from the benefit profiles.

best practice

A defined and proven method of managing events effectively.

boundary

The scope of what a programme will cover; the extent of its influence and authority.

business change manager (BCM)

The role responsible for benefits management, from identification through to realization, and for ensuring that the implementation and embedding of the new capabilities are delivered by the projects. Typically allocated to more than one individual and also known as 'change agent'.

business change team

A group of specialists appointed to support a business change manager in the business change management aspects of benefits realization.

capability

The completed set of project outputs required to deliver an outcome; this exists prior to transition. It is a service, function or operation that enables the organization to exploit opportunities.

configuration

A generic term used to describe a group of products or items that work together to deliver a product or service, or a recognizable part of a product or service. A configuration may be a configuration item of a larger configuration.

configuration management

Technical and administrative activities concerned with the creation, maintenance and controlled change of configuration throughout the life of a product.

consult

To give groups or individuals the opportunity to contribute to and make recommendations on an action or document.

corporate portfolio

The totality of the change initiatives within an organization; it may comprise a number of programmes, standalone projects and other initiatives that achieve congruence of change.

dependency

An activity, output or decision that is required to achieve some aspect of the programme. It can be internal or external to the programme.

dis-benefit

A measurable decline resulting from an outcome perceived as negative by one or more stakeholders, which reduces one or more organizational objective(s).

emergent programme

A programme that subsumes one or more pre-existing projects into a coherent alignment with corporate policy and strategy.

end goal

The ultimate objective of a programme – the same as the 'to-be state' or 'future state'.

gated review

A structured review of a project, programme or portfolio as part of formal governance arrangements carried out at key decision points in the lifecycle to ensure that the decision to invest as per the agreed business case remains valid.

governance

The functions, responsibilities, processes and procedures that define how a programme is set up, managed and controlled.

inform

In the context of a RACI table, to advise a group or individual of a change or a decision. In MSP, this is typically used in the context of something that affects activities or document creation.

issue

A relevant event that has happened, was not planned and requires management action. It could be a problem, query, concern, change request or risk that has occurred.

leadership

The ability to direct, influence and motivate others towards a better outcome.

margin

The flexibility that a programme has for achieving its blueprint, benefits and business case.

opportunity

An uncertain event that could have a favourable impact on objectives or benefits.

outcome

The result of change, normally affecting real-world behaviour or circumstances. Outcomes are desired when a change is conceived. Outcomes are achieved as a result of the activities undertaken to effect the change; they are the manifestation of part or all of the new state conceived in the blueprint.

output

The tangible or intangible artefact produced, constructed or created as a result of a planned activity.

P3M3

The Portfolio, Programme and Project Management Maturity Model that provides a framework with which organizations can assess their current performance and put in place improvement plans.

plan

A detailed proposal for doing or achieving something, detailing the what, when, how and by whom.

portfolio

The totality of an organization's investment (or segment thereof) in the changes required to achieve its strategic objectives.

product

An input or output, whether tangible or intangible, that can be described in advance, created and tested; also known as an output or deliverable.

programme

A temporary flexible organization structure created to coordinate, direct and oversee the implementation of a set of related projects and activities in order to deliver outcomes and benefits related to an organization's strategic objectives. A programme is likely to have a life that spans several years.

programme assurance

Independent assessment and confirmation that the programme as a whole or any one of its aspects are on track, that it is applying relevant practices and procedures, and that the projects, activities and business rationale remain aligned to the programme's objectives. *See also* gated review.

programme board

A group that is established to support a senior responsible owner (SRO) in delivering a programme.

programme management

The coordinated organization, direction and implementation of a dossier of projects and transformation activities (i.e. the programme) to achieve outcomes and realize benefits of strategic importance.

programme manager

The role responsible for the set-up, management and delivery of a programme; typically allocated to a single individual.

programme office

The function providing the information hub and standards custodian for a programme and its delivery objectives; it could provide support for more than one programme.

programme organization

How a programme will be managed throughout its lifecycle, the roles and responsibilities of individuals involved in the programme, and personnel management or human resources arrangements. Also known as programme organization structure.

project

A temporary organization that is created for the purpose of delivering one or more business outputs according to a specified business case.

quality

The degree to which the features and inherent or assigned characteristics of a product, person, process, service and/or system bear on its ability to show that it meets expectations or stated needs, requirements or specification.

quality control

The process of monitoring specific results to determine whether they comply with the relevant standards and identifying ways to eliminate causes of unsatisfactory performance.

quality management system (QMS)

The complete set of quality standards, procedures and responsibilities for a site or organization.

register

A formal repository that is managed and requires agreement by the board on its format, composition and use.

responsible

Used to describe the individual who has the authority and is expected to deliver a task or activity; responsibility can be delegated.

risk

An uncertain event or set of events that, should it occur, will have an effect on the achievement of objectives. A risk is measured by a combination of the probability of a perceived threat or opportunity occurring and the magnitude of its impact on objectives.

risk assessment

The identification and evaluation of risks.

risk management

The systematic application of principles, approaches and processes to the tasks of identifying and assessing risks, and then planning and implementing risk responses.

senior responsible owner (SRO)

The single individual with overall responsibility for ensuring that a project or programme meets its objectives and delivers the projected benefits.

sponsor

The main driving force behind a programme or project. Some organizations use the term sponsor instead of SRO.

sponsoring group

The driving force behind a programme, which provides the investment decision and top-level endorsement for the rationale and objectives of the programme.

stakeholder

Any individual, group or organization that can affect, be affected by, or perceives itself to be affected by, a programme.

stakeholder map

A diagrammatic representation of the stakeholders relevant to an organizational activity and their respective interests.

strategy

An approach or line to take, designed to achieve a long-term aim. Strategies can exist at different levels in an organization – in MSP there are corporate strategies for achieving objectives that will give rise to programmes. Programmes then develop strategies aligned with these corporate objectives against particular delivery areas.

threat

An uncertain event that could have a negative impact on objectives or benefits.

to-be state

The future planned state of an organization as described by the blueprint.

tranche

A programme management term describing a group of projects structured around distinct step changes in capability and benefit delivery.

transformation

A distinct change to the way an organization conducts all or part of its business.

vision

A picture of a better future that will be delivered by the programme.

workstream

The logical grouping of projects and activities that together enable effective management. Workstreams may delineate projects against a variety of criteria.

Index

Index